VEGETARIAN COOKING FOR CHILDREN

VEGETARIAN COOKING FOR CHILDREN

Rosamond Richardson

PIATKUS

For Emily, Nicholas and William, with love

© 1986 Rosamond Richardson

First published in 1986 by
Judy Piatkus (Publishers) Limited of
5 Windmill Street, London W.1.

British Library Cataloguing in Publication Data

Richardson, Rosamond
   Vegetarian cooking for children.
   I. Cookery (Vegetables)
   I. Title
   641.6'5 TX801

ISBN 0–86188–580–5
ISBN 0–86188–958–4 (pbk)

Edited by Susan Fleming
Designed and illustrated by Paul Saunders

Phototypeset in 11/13 pt Linotron Plantin
Printed and bound in Great Britain at
The Bath Press, Bath, Avon

CONTENTS

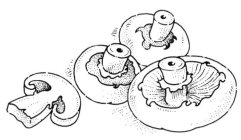

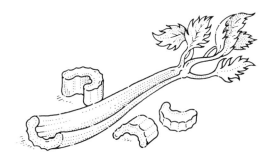

INTRODUCTION

An increasing interest in vegetarianism over recent years has intrigued many young people, even very young children, some of whom are becoming committed and thinking vegetarians. This immediately presents problems within the family: how does the cook in the household, usually the mother, cope with providing vegetarian meals for one element, meat meals for another, and retain her sanity? Fortunately for her, there has been quite a trend away from eating the traditional 'meat and two veg' every day, and meals of pasta, soufflés, or rice dishes are perfectly normal and acceptable family fare. But still some problems remain and it is not easy to make the adjustment to integrating vegetarian concepts into the family. Yet it is not impossible, and indeed can be an interesting and enjoyable challenge.

Children become vegetarian for a number of different reasons. Some instinctively hate the idea of killing animals and eating them: they are repulsed by 'humane' slaughterhouse methods, upset by the idea of factory farming, and as soon as they know that sausages are made up of the leftover lips, eyelids and other revolting scraps off the corpse, nothing would prevail upon them ever to eat another one. Others turn vegetarian for reasons of health: they might be allergic to certain foods, perhaps they believe that it is better for their general health, or they may wish to reduce their body weight and stay fit and slim. Apart from these considerations, many children actually *prefer* the taste of vegetarian food – when a vegetarian dish is offered as an alternative in schools, for example, it is very often the first to disappear. Another good reason for turning vegetarian is one of economy, although that is more likely to be held in consideration by the adults in the family: the price of meat alone is enough to encourage a vegetarian shopping basket!

The first question that many parents ask when the possibility arises of a vegetarian in the family is, is it a healthy diet? Where do they get their protein? The answer is that it *can* be a far healthier diet than a meat-based one, and there is no lack of protein so long as you provide wholemeal bread, nuts, pulses, cheese and other dairy produce. And since there is a link in many people's minds between wholefoods and vegetarianism, the chances are that the diet will be free of many of the additives, preservatives and other toxins found in processed and convenience foods which are so widely eaten. One of the virtues of vegetarianism is that it is a thinking person's way, and nothing but good can come of an increased awareness of what we are eating, and what we are doing to obtain it. We should be delighted that our children show leanings towards vegetarianism!

In order to help ensure that you are giving your child or children a nutritious and well-balanced diet, there are tables in the front of the book which are a guide to all the good sources of dietary fibre, protein, fats, carbohydrates, vitamins and minerals. As you use them, do give a thought also to what you are giving your children to drink: so many of the convenience beverages are full of sugar and harmful additives, and they are expensive. And children are often just as happy with a glass of water – especially if it has an ice cube or two in it!

I have found, in my own experience of feeding three young children, that giving fun names to the food helps enormously in their enjoyment of it, and it's also a good idea to decorate the dishes wittily from time to time. Children are very conservative about their food on the whole, but both these devices serve to beguile even the most dubious and sceptical of youngsters. I remember once giving my boys yam – slivered and fried until it was golden, quite wonderful – but I decided to call it something else with a jolly title, and they loved it. Afterwards I told them what it was and they were aghast – they would never have eaten it had I told the whole truth and nothing but the truth. Now they love yam! Yet at the same time nothing can disguise things that they don't like, and none of the kids that I have tried them out on have ever liked meat substitutes. They won't be fooled, either by the taste or by the appearance, and it is insulting to their intelligence to expect them to be. Rather, the approach I take in this book will show that nobody need to think in terms of meat substitutes, but rather of producing composite foods of variety and interest, which are good to look at, to smell and to taste. On the other hand, some of the instant vegetarian convenience foods – sausage mixes, vegeburger mixes and so on – have proved very popular and are well worth having in the store-cupboard for when time is short and inspiration at a low ebb.

If you are a vegetarian yourself and want to bring up your children that way, it is obviously best to start them as young as possible, because so much of our eating is based on habit. Make it fun for them – and don't be *too* dogmatic, for forbidden fruit is dangerously attractive! Practising what you preach is important, too, so it is only fair to buy what you want your children to eat, and keep temptation out of their way. Above all, eating vegetarian food with a young family should be a source of pleasure and satisfaction, not a penance. You will find that the most committed of meat-eaters in the family will enjoy these meals enormously, and indeed may not even notice that they are not eating meat!

Recipes marked with a ★ can be made by children themselves (sometimes with a little help from Mum!).

A BALANCED DIET

A healthy and balanced diet for your children means ensuring a daily supply for them of dietary fibre, protein, carbohydrates and fats, minerals and vitamins. A good balance will give them ample energy – but not too much, for otherwise this is stored in the form of excess fat. The protein question is always the first to be raised by people enquiring into vegetarianism, and it is easily answered: there is no shortage of protein in a sensible vegetarian diet. All the pulses and grains have a high protein content, as do nuts, peas, cheese and other dairy produce. And these proteins are actually superior to the animal proteins in meat because the latter contain high levels of uric acid: the liver frequently finds itself unable to cope with these levels, and the remainder is deposited in the joints which then become stiff and eventually arthritic.

Many of the most nutritious of vegetarian meals are extremely simple: wholemeal bread and cheese, or rice with beans, or cereals with milk, provide wholesome and balanced meals well stocked with protein as well as all the other daily requirements. One of the myths about protein is the level required for daily consumption – it is nothing like so high as some people think. The latest World Health Organisation recommendation is for between 25–50 g (1–2 oz) per day as the level required to maintain and replace body tissue.

Good sources of Protein	**Good sources of Dietary Fibre**
Flour and bread: wholewheat, soya and rye	Bran and oatmeal, muesli
Yeast extract	Dried fruits
Bran and oatmeal, muesli	Nuts and desiccated coconut
Parmesan, Cheddar, Brie and cottage cheeses	Flours: wholewheat and soya
All nuts	Wholewheat bread
Eggs	Parsley
Lentils and chick peas: pulses generally	Haricot beans: pulses generally
Peas, spinach, sweetcorn	Raspberries
Milk and dried milk	Spinach, sweetcorn
Dried apricots	Olives

Good Sources of Vitamins

Vitamin A

carrots
parsley
spinach
butter
dried apricots
watercress
broccoli
Cheddar cheese,
    etc.
melon
mango
eggs
milk

Vitamin B$_1$

yeast extract
Brazil nuts
peanuts
bran
oatmeal
wholewheat flour
rye flour
wholewheat
    bread
peas

Vitamin B$_2$

almonds
Brie cheese, etc.
Cheddar cheese
Parmesan cheese
wholewheat flour
dried peaches
mushrooms
wholewheat
    bread
dried apricots
broad beans
dates

Vitamin B$_3$

yeast extract
peanuts
yeast
wholewheat flour
dried peaches
mushrooms
wholewheat bread
dried apricots
broad beans
dates

Vitamin B$_6$

bran
yeast extract
hazelnuts
bananas
wholewheat
    flour
peanuts
avocado pear
currants
Brussels sprouts
    (raw)
prunes
cauliflower
    (raw)

Vitamin B$_{12}$

egg yolk
Cheddar cheese
yeast extract
Parmesan cheese
Brie cheese
milk
cream
cottage cheese
yogurt
butter

Folic acid

yeast
yeast extract
bran
spinach
broccoli
peanuts
Brussels sprouts
    (raw)
almonds
cabbage (raw)
peas (cooked)
hazelnuts
avocado pear

Vitamin C

red and green
    peppers
blackcurrants
parsley
lemon
watercress
cabbage (raw)
strawberries
cauliflower (raw)
oranges
grapefruit
lychees
broccoli (cooked)
mangoes
radishes
raspberries
spinach (cooked)

Vitamin D

eggs   cheese
butter   margarine
sunlight enables the body
to make Vitamin D in the skin

Vitamin E

almost all foods

Vitamin K

green vegetables

Pantothenic acid

all foods

There are many other guidelines for a balanced diet. Buy fresh food whenever possible, because tired or over-ripe ingredients have a greatly reduced vitamin content. Try not to overcook food, and give children lots of raw food – many kids actually prefer raw to cooked carrots, for example. Try to avoid giving them refined or processed foods, where possible, as these often contain additives and preservatives which have uncertain effects on our children's health. Try not to overdo the sugary foods like sweets, chocolate and biscuits, and avoid canned drinks wherever possible. Try not to give them too much fat – beware of the crisp packet even when it says 'low fat' – but rather give them high energy foods like bread, cheese and nuts. And to end a meal, pass around the yogurt and fresh fruit bowl, so that cooked puddings become the exception rather than the rule – a treat to look forward to. Having said that, it is also important to repeat that you must not be *too* dogmatic – because otherwise you will have a family of rebels on your hands! Make it fun, and relax about the occasional convenience-food meal – it won't kill them if the basic elements for their daily diet are carefully thought out, and providing them with a wholesome and healthy life-style.

The Vitamins and their Functions

Vitamin A: Maintains the cells in the cornea of the eye.

B Vitamins:
B_1 (Thiamine). Essential for the metabolism of carbohydrates.
B_2 (Riboflavin). For respiration and maintaining eye cells.
B_3 (Niacin). For the metabolism of carbohydrates.
B_6 (Pyridoxine). Essential for metabolism.
B_{12} (Cyanocobalamine). For making red blood cells.
Folic acid. For metabolism of proteins and making red blood cells.
Biotin. For metabolism.

Vitamin C (Ascorbic acid):   For the metabolism of foods. Helps absorption of iron. Makes collagen which bonds the cells of the body together, and connective tissue.

Vitamin D: For absorption of calcium and phosphorus by the bones and teeth.

Vitamin E: Important for nerve function.

Vitamin K: Essential for normal blood-clotting.

BASIC FOODS

When you are changing or developing a new style of cooking, some of the basic ingredients require re-thinking – so here is a wide variety of handy hints for what to have on hand (and why!), and how to cope with preparing and cooking rice and pulses.

creatures all converted to a jelly by long boiling. Since this information never fails to revolt children, use agar-agar instead – it is derived from seaweed and does the same work as gelatine. You can obtain it from most health-food stores.

Fats and Oils in Cooking

In general it is best to use vegetable oils in cooking – it makes for lighter and healthier food. Where the recipe indicates margarine try to obtain one high in polyunsaturates, and use butter sparingly in cooking. Where you can, grill food instead of frying it.

You will find from experience which oils your children prefer – sunflower, safflower, groundnut, olive and mixed vegetable oils are on the shelves of most supermarkets. Sunflower oil is our favourite – it contains the same amino acid as Evening Primrose oil so I always feel that I am getting an elixir as well as a bargain!

When you are buying frozen pastry, do look out for one made with vegetable oils instead of animal fats – they are available, so it is well worth stopping to read the label.

Gelatine

Gelatine is an animal product. It consists of the skins, tendons and ligaments of various

Eggs

Use free-range eggs – they taste better and you are doing the chickens a favour by supporting humane farming methods.

Milk

Use low-fat skimmed milk for preference.

Salt and Pepper

Use natural salts such as sea salt or rock salt, but keep the salt content of your cooking low. If you are very salt-conscious cut it out altogether and use lemon juice for flavouring instead, or small amounts of tamari or soy sauce. Yeast extract is excellent for flavouring, too, and is a good source of the B vitamins.

Unless otherwise stated, the pepper in the recipes is freshly ground black pepper. It has far more flavour than ready-ground pepper which is insipid by comparison and tends to lose its heat on storage.

Herbs and Spices

The success of vegetarian food is partly dependent on the thoughtful use of herbs and spices – so introduce them gradually to your children when they are very young, and they will come to love them. Used in moderation they will even eat garlic and enjoy it – so make the food smell and taste as good as possible, and they will never change from vegetarian fare!

Pulse	Soak	Cook
Split peas, mung beans, red lentils	2 hrs	15 mins
Green and brown lentils	6 hrs	20–30 mins
Chick peas, haricot beans	8 hrs	30 mins
Aduki, flageolets, cannellini	8 hrs	20–25 mins
Black-eyed beans, soy beans	10 hrs	30–40 mins
Black beans	10 hrs	1 hr
Kidney beans	10 hrs	1½ hrs

COOKING PULSES

There used to be a great mystique about cooking pulses: 'Oh, but you have to soak them overnight, and how do you remember to do that?' However, that is not very different from remembering to defrost something, and preparing pulses – leaving them to soak in cold water to cover them – becomes, like many other things, a habit. The small pulses like mung beans, lentils and split peas require only a few hours' soaking, whereas the larger ones – butter beans, haricots, black-eyed beans, kidney beans etc – must be soaked overnight.

Drain off the soaking water and put the pulses into a saucepan. Add dried herbs, a bay leaf and a small onion to the pan. Cover with water, and bring to the boil. Simmer, covered with a lid, for the required time (see the table below). About 5 minutes before the end of the cooking, season with a little sea salt and pepper if required: salt will harden the skins of the pulses if added earlier. Finally drain the cooked pulses and they are ready to use.

COOKING RICE

For four people, use 2 teacups white rice and 3 teacups water. Bring to simmering point and stir. Add salt if desired, then cover with a lid, turn the heat down and steam the rice until all the liquid is absorbed, about 20 minutes. Remove from the heat and rest until ready to serve. On no account disturb the rice after the preliminary stirring.

Brown or wild rice requires longer simmering to cook through properly. Cover the rice with a generous amount of water and bring to the boil. Add salt if desired and simmer, covered, for 35–40 minutes until cooked, when it will be tender but still slightly crunchy. Drain and serve.

COOKING PASTA

Most commercial pasta requires a fairly short cooking time, which will be given in the instructions on the packet. Pasta is not appetising if it is overcooked and soggy: it is best when, although tender and cooked through, it still retains a bit of bite – as the Italians have it, '*al dente*'.

VEGETABLE STOCK

You can either make your own vegetable stock from vegetable trimmings and potato peelings etc (see below), or you can buy vegetable stock cubes from many health-food stores.

Using vegetables such as onions, carrots, leeks, cabbage, tomatoes, Jerusalem artichokes etc – and leftover potato peelings too – makes the best of whatever is in season, or of leftovers. Put them into a large saucepan and cover with water. Add salt, peppercorns and bay leaves for flavouring, and either fresh or dried herbs according to the time of year. Bring to the boil and simmer, covered, for 1 hour. Leave to stand until cold, then strain. Keep chilled for up to 5 days. Alternatively, this stock freezes very well.

TO BAKE BLIND

Line the prepared pastry case with a sheet of oil and fill it with dried beans – kidney beans for example – reserving these beans for this purpose for future use since they will be rendered inedible! Bake in a pre-heated oven at 325°F/160°C/Gas 3 for 10–15 minutes, then remove the foil and return the pastry to the oven for a further 5 minutes or so, just to crisp it up.

CRISPY PASTRY

175 g (6 oz) plain flour
$\frac{1}{2}$ teaspoon salt
2 tablespoons sesame seeds
5 tablespoons vegetable oil
$1\frac{1}{2}$ tablespoons water

Sieve the flour with the salt and stir in the sesame seeds, oil and water. Mix well and knead briefly until smooth. Press into a greased 20 cm (8 inch) flan dish with your knuckles, and bake blind without chilling. Use for savoury dishes.

BLENDER PASTRY

75 g (3 oz) soft margarine
175 g (6 oz) plain flour
3 tablespoons water
a large pinch of salt

Put all the ingredients into the blender and blend until they have formed a dough. Knead to a smooth ball and chill. Bake blind before using.

POTATO PASTRY

250 g (8 oz) potatoes, peeled and cooked
50 g (2 oz) margarine
salt to taste
125 g (4 oz) flour
1 teaspoon baking powder
25 g (1 oz) cheese, finely grated (optional)

13

Mash the potatoes thoroughly with the margarine and add salt to taste. Sift the flour with the baking powder and mix in thoroughly. Chill, then roll out on a floured board as for ordinary pastry. Bake blind before using.

SIMPLE SWEET PASTRY

75 g (3 oz) caster sugar
150 g (5 oz) margarine or butter, melted
250 g (8 oz) plain flour, sifted

Add the sugar to the melted fat and stir over a gentle heat until dissolved. Stir in the sifted flour and work to a smooth dough. Chill. Press into a 25 cm (10 inch), well-greased flan tin, and bake blind.

BÉCHAMEL

40 g (1½ oz) butter or margarine
2 tablespoons flour
300 ml (½ pint) milk, warmed
salt and pepper

Melt the butter or margarine in a thick-bottomed pan and stir in the flour with a wooden spoon. Add the milk slowly, stirring all the time until the sauce thickens. Season to taste, and simmer over a very gentle heat for 5-8 minutes, and thin out with more milk if necessary.

VINAIGRETTE

2 tablespoons lemon juice
2 teaspoons French mustard
salt and pepper
garlic to taste, crushed (optional)
150 ml (¼ pint) olive oil

Mix the lemon juice into the mustard and season with salt and pepper. Add the crushed garlic, if using. Stir in the olive oil gradually, stirring thoroughly all the time, until the mixture thickens and amalgamates. Leave to stand for a while before using so that the flavours blend.

MAYONNAISE

1 free-range egg
1 teaspoon dry mustard
salt and pepper
300 ml (½ pint) vegetable oil, such as sunflower

Put the egg into the food processor and add the mustard, salt and pepper. Liquidize, then begin to pour in a thin stream of oil, with the machine still working. Stop pouring from time to time to let the mixture thicken – and be careful not to pour too fast right at the beginning otherwise the mixture will separate. When the oil is used up, check the seasoning and transfer to a screw-top jar. Refrigerate until ready to use.

GARLIC MAYONNAISE

Crush the amount of garlic you require into the mayonnaise above about 30 minutes before serving. It is best eaten within 24 hours since the garlic tends to turn the mayonnaise rancid after a longer period of time.

BLUE CHEESE MAYONNAISE

To the mayonnaise above add 50–75 g (2–3 oz) blue cheese, thoroughly mashed. Blend the two together in the food processor and store in the refrigerator in a screw-top jar.

BLUE CHEESE DRESSING

50 g (2 oz) blue cheese, mashed
150 ml (¼ pint) vinaigrette (see page 14)
garlic to taste, crushed (optional)

Stir the cheese into the vinaigrette and blend them together thoroughly, with the garlic if using. You can do this in the liquidizer if you like, for a really smooth, creamy dressing.

RASPBERRY AND SOY SAUCE DRESSING

5 tablespoons raspberry vinegar (see page 16)
1–2 tablespoons soy sauce, to taste
garlic to taste, crushed (optional)

Simply mix the two liquids together and add garlic to taste if you want. It is a sublime dressing – very popular with the children, and so easily prepared!

GREEN HERB DRESSING

3 tablespoons mixed fresh herbs, finely chopped
2 soft-boiled eggs, peeled
150 ml (¼ pint) vinaigrette (see page 14)
sea salt and pepper

Blend all the ingredients together in the food processor and season to taste. This is delicious on salads of all kinds – pasta, beans, mushroom or vegetable (see the range on pages 65–69).

YOGURT VINAIGRETTE

150 ml (¼ pint) vinaigrette (see page 14)
1 small carton natural yogurt

Stir the vinaigrette into the yogurt until smooth and creamy, and it is ready to serve! It is really delicious on tomato salad, and excellent with coleslaw.

YOGURT HERB DRESSING

4 tablespoons mixed fresh herbs, finely chopped
2 spring onions, finely sliced
2 hard-boiled eggs, very finely chopped
5 tablespoons vinaigrette (see page 14)
1 small carton natural yogurt
salt and pepper

Mix the chopped herbs, spring onions and hard-boiled eggs into the vinaigrette and blend thoroughly. Stir in the yogurt until well amalgamated, and season to taste with salt and pepper.

RASPBERRY VINEGAR

750 g (1½ lb) raspberries, washed
water
1.2 litres (2 pints) malt vinegar
1 kg (2 lb) sugar

Cover the raspberries with water in a large pan and bring to the boil. Simmer gently for 30 minutes, covered. Then strain off the juice and mix it with the vinegar and sugar. Stir over a gentle heat until the sugar has dissolved, then bring to the boil again and simmer for 10 minutes or so until it becomes syrupy. Store in clean, screw-top bottles.
Makes 3 litres (5 pints).

GARLIC CROÛTONS

FOR 4
4 medium slices bread, crusts removed
sunflower oil, for frying
1–2 cloves of garlic, crushed

Cut the crustless slices of bread into tiny cubes. Heat the oil gently and fry the bread over a medium heat, shaking regularly to turn them, until they begin to crisp up. Then turn the heat down and add the crushed garlic to the pan. Continue cooking, stirring the croûtons constantly, for a further couple of minutes so that the garlic flavour permeates them, but being careful that the garlic itself does not burn. Remove from the pan and drain on kitchen paper. Keep in a warm oven until ready to use.

SCRUMPTIOUS SOUPS

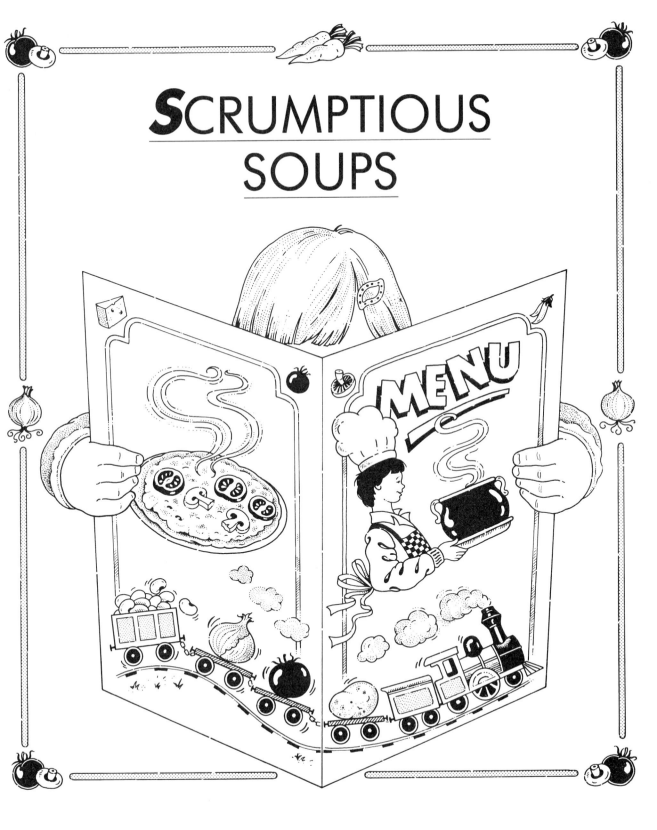

Soups are satisfying, nourishing food which I find very popular with my hungry family – and they have the advantage of being simple to prepare and serve. Dished up with a basket of fresh wholemeal rolls or a loaf of warm, crusty granary bread, these make light meals in themselves. Followed by cheese and fresh fruit, the nutritional balance is perfect – and the cook is not exhausted!

TOMATO NOODLE SOUP ★

This light, aromatic soup is a great favourite with my family and we often have it as a simple lunch, with lots of fresh bread and interesting cheese to follow. Finally the fruit bowl – what could be easier?

FOR 4–6

750 g (1½ lb) tomatoes, skinned and
   chopped, *or*
   1 × 500 g (1 lb) can tomatoes
3 tablespoons vegetable oil
1 medium onion, chopped
1 small bunch parsley, chopped

1 tablespoon mixed dried herbs
600 ml (1 pint) stock
125 g (4 oz) vermicelli, soaked in hot
   water for 5 minutes
grated Parmesan cheese, to garnish

Cook the tomatoes in the oil for 5 minutes, stirring until they become very soft. Then mix in the onion, parsley and dried herbs and simmer for 10 minutes, stirring occasionally. Add the stock and simmer for a further 5 minutes. Liquidize, and season to taste. Finally stir in the cooked vermicelli, heat through and serve with a bowl of grated Parmesan on the table, to sprinkle over the top of each serving.

Secret Soup

The secret of the soup is that nobody can ever guess the basic ingredient. The cannellini beans, puréed with the other vegetables, make a thick and nourishing base which is slightly creamy in texture. Another good cold-weather soup.

FOR 6

2 large onions, chopped
6 stalks celery, sliced
2 large carrots, sliced,
3 tablespoons vegetable oil
900 ml (1½ pints) stock

250 g (8 oz) canned cannellini beans, drained
1 large bunch parsley, chopped
salt and pepper

Simmer the sliced vegetables in the oil for 10 minutes, turning frequently, then cover with the stock and simmer until tender, about another 10 minutes. Add the beans and parsley to the mixture and liquidize. Season to taste and serve piping hot.

Best Watercress Soup

The very special flavour of watercress makes a delicious soup, which is also a very pretty green. It makes a lovely starter at suppertime.

FOR 4

500 g (1 lb) carrots, sliced
2 large onions, peeled and chopped
3 tablespoons olive oil
900 ml (1½ pints) stock

2 bunches watercress
150 ml (¼ pint) milk
sea salt

Soften the carrots and onions in the oil over a gentle heat, stirring frequently. Then pour on the stock and simmer for 10 minutes. Stir in the watercress and cook for a further minute or two, then liquidize the soup. Thin out with the milk, season to taste with sea salt and it is ready to serve.

CHEESE SOUP

Nutritious and substantial, this is a fabulous cold-weather soup to warm you through on wintry days. The cheese makes it thick and creamy and, served with warm granary bread, it is a satisfying meal in itself.

FOR 4

250 g (8 oz) potatoes, peeled
250 g (8 oz) onions, peeled and sliced
125 g (4 oz) carrots, sliced
900 ml (1½ pints) stock (see page 13)

175 g (6 oz) mature Cheddar cheese, grated
salt and pepper
chopped parsley, to garnish

Boil all the vegetables in the stock until soft, about 12 minutes. Liquidize. Return to the heat and stir in the cheese until it melts. Thin out with more stock or milk if necessary, check the seasoning, and serve garnished with chopped parsley.

GOLDEN SWEETCORN SOUP

A really heavenly dish, especially if you use fresh sweetcorn. To me it is a soup of late summer when corn-cobs are plentiful. Golden and irresistible, the soup has a marvellous texture given it by a single egg white. No leftovers in my family!

FOR 4

350 g (12 oz) sweetcorn kernels cut off the cob, *or*
1 × 350 g (12 oz) can sweetcorn, drained
600 ml (1 pint) stock or milk
8–10 spring onions, finely chopped

75 g (3 oz) button mushrooms, finely sliced
1 tablespoon vegetable oil
salt and pepper
1 egg white
chopped parsley, to garnish

Simmer the sweetcorn in the stock or milk for 10–15 minutes if fresh, 8–10 minutes if canned. Liquidize. Add the spring onions and mushrooms and cook for another 5 minutes. Add the oil and seasoning to taste. Whisk the egg white until very stiff and fold into the soup, stirring thoroughly. When it begins to thicken, transfer to a tureen and garnish with chopped parsley.

CREAMY LENTIL SOUP

I have found this a useful way of accustoming children to lentils. They are conservative creatures, and often pre-conditioned to dislike new ingredients. But this really delicious purée of lentils and vegetables has converted many a child at my table!

FOR 6

250 g (8 oz) green lentils, soaked
1 large onion, thickly sliced
2 bay leaves
1 tablespoon dried herbs
4 celery stalks, sliced

3 medium carrots, sliced
125 g (4 oz) low-fat curd cheese
milk, if necessary
nutmeg, salt and pepper

Drain the lentils and cover with fresh water. Bring to the boil with the onion, bay leaves and dried herbs, and simmer for 25 minutes, adding the celery and carrots for the last 10 minutes of the cooking. Remove the bay leaves and liquidize the soup to a thick purée. Mix a little of this into the curd cheese until well-blended, then add to the soup and liquidize again. Thin out with a little milk if necessary and season to taste with salt and pepper. Serve hot.

MARVELLOUS
MAIN COURSES

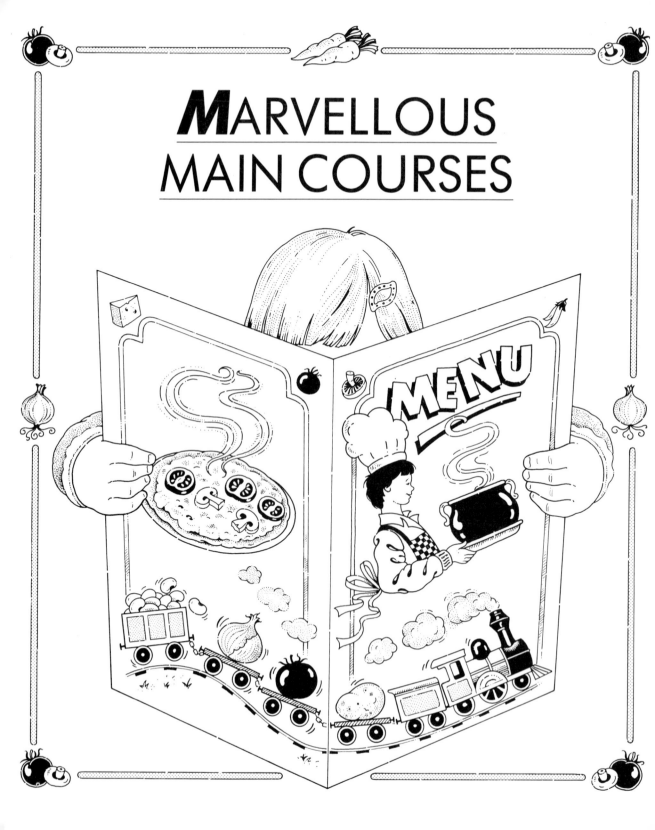

Many people tend to think of vegetarian main courses as being very limited – and, dare one say it, boring. But the range of pasta, pizzas, egg dishes, loaves, pastry delicacies and scrumptious cheese recipes is enormous, and anything but dull. The kids will never tire of them, and it is food for all seasons.

BUBBLING CASSEROLE ★

A scrumptious lunch dish, easy to prepare and always gobbled up by my responsive family, these crunchy layers of nuts and celery and macaroni are irresistibly topped with a bubbling cheese sauce.

FOR 4

250 g (8 oz) macaroni, cooked 'al dente'
1 small head of celery, very finely shredded
125 g (4 oz) dry-roasted peanuts, roughly chopped

250 g (8 oz) Cheddar cheese, grated
300 ml (½ pint) béchamel (see page 14)
salt and pepper

Make a layer of all the macaroni in the bottom of a well-greased ovenproof dish. (To vary this recipe you could use an equivalent quantity of baked beans instead.) Cover with the shredded celery and top this layer with the roughly chopped peanuts. Add the grated cheese to the béchamel and melt it over a gentle heat. Season to taste, and pour over the top of the dish. Bake in a preheated oven at 350°F/180°C/Gas 4 until the casserole is bubbly, about 20-25 minutes.

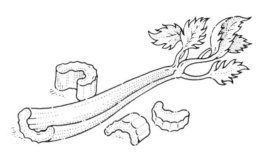

MERRY MUSHROOM LOAF

The vegetarian 'loaf' is a versatile stand-by for a central feature of a main course. There are countless variations that you can experiment with, but here is a master recipe on which to base other ideas. Light and well-seasoned, this should satisfy the most critical of carnivores in the family!

FOR 4–6

1 medium onion, chopped
250 g (8 oz) mushrooms, sliced
2 garlic cloves, crushed (optional)
2 tablespoons vegetable oil
4 medium carrots, grated

3 eggs, beaten
25 g (1 oz) wholemeal breadcrumbs
50 g (2 oz) Cheddar cheese, grated
1 tablespoon fresh herbs, chopped
salt, pepper and a pinch of allspice

Cook the onion, mushrooms and garlic (if used) in the oil for 5–6 minutes in a heavy pan. Season to taste, then mix in a bowl with the carrots and beaten eggs. Mix the breadcrumbs, cheese and herbs together and divide into two portions. Add one-half to the vegetable mixture and pour into a greased loaf tin of 750 g (1½ lb) capacity. Spread the remaining cheese mixture over the top and bake at 300°F/150°C/Gas 2 for 1 hour. Leave to cool in the tin for at least 10 minutes, then turn out and serve warm or cold.

TOPPING TOMATO LAYERS ★

Simplicity itself, this is one the quickest of main-course dishes to make, and you can try seasoning it quite liberally with garlic and spices if your family like them, just to add zest and extra interest.

FOR 4

4 large tomatoes, skinned and
    chopped
75 g (3 oz) fresh granary breadcrumbs
175 g (6 oz) button mushrooms,
    chopped

75 g (3 oz) Cheddar or Edam cheese,
    finely grated
salt and pepper
25 g (1 oz) margarine or butter

Grease an ovenproof dish. Make layers in it of tomatoes, breadcrumbs, mushrooms and cheese until all the ingredients are used up, ending with a final layer of breadcrumbs. Season as you go. Dot with butter or margarine and bake at 325°F/160°C/Gas 3 for 30 minutes.

LEEK PASTIES WITH MUSHROOM SAUCE

These leeks wrapped in pastry are astonishingly delicious for something so simple. The creamy mushroom sauce is a perfect accompaniment, and makes this a meal to remember.

FOR 6

1 × 250 g (8 oz) packet puff pastry
6 medium leeks, cooked and chopped
1 egg yolk, beaten

FOR THE SAUCE

250 g (8 oz) mushrooms, chopped
25 g (1 oz) margarine or butter
150 ml ($\frac{1}{4}$ pint) single cream
salt and pepper
300 ml ($\frac{1}{2}$ pint) béchamel (see page 14)

Roll out the pastry thinly and cut into six squares about 13 cm (5 inches) square. Divide the chopped leek between each square and fold the pastry over to form a triangle, sealing it by moistening the inside edges with water and pressing down with a fork. Brush with beaten egg yolk and bake in a preheated oven at 400°F/200°C/Gas 6 for 15–18 minutes until puffed and golden.

To make the sauce, sauté the mushrooms in the margarine or butter, add the cream and simmer for 3–4 minutes so that it reduces a little. Season to taste and stir into the béchamel. Liquidize all together, then reheat and serve hot with the leek pasties.

CRUNCHY CROUSTADES ★

There are very many variations that you can try out on a theme of hollowed-out bread rolls. They make excellent vehicles for all kinds of creamed fillings, and of course you can use the scooped-out insides for breadcrumbs so that nothing is wasted.

FOR 4

6 round granary bread rolls cut in half

FOR THE FILLING

500 g (1 lb) cooked vegetables (peas, mushrooms, broccoli, leeks, sweetcorn, mangetouts, French beans, baby carrots etc)

450 ml ($\frac{3}{4}$ pint) béchamel (see page 14)
salt and pepper
2 tablespoons grated Parmesan cheese
2 egg whites, beaten very stiffly

Remove the crumbs from the bread rolls so that each half is hollow. Chop the cooked vegetables where necessary, and mix into the béchamel. Season with salt and pepper and spoon the filling into the bread cases. Fold the Parmesan into the beaten egg whites and top each croustade with a little of this mixture, smoothing it over the filling. Bake in a preheated oven at 400°F/200°C/Gas 6 for 10–12 minutes until the topping is puffed and golden.

SAVOURY SPRING ROLLS

My children – along with all their friends – love things made with pastry, and these mouth-watering rolls with their simple filling of cheese and spring onions are a regular favourite in this household.

FOR 4

1 × 250 g (8 oz) packet puff pastry, defrosted
1 bunch spring onions, chopped
2 tablespoons dried herbs

125 g (4 oz) Cheddar cheese, finely grated
1 egg, beaten

Roll the pastry out thinly and cut into oblongs about 10×5 cm (4×2 inches). Mix the spring onions and herbs into the grated cheese and mix with half of the beaten egg. Spoon one-eighth of this mixture lengthwise on to each piece of pastry, and roll it up like a sausage roll, sealing the seam with water. Place seam-side down on a well greased baking sheet, and brush with the remaining beaten egg. Bake in a preheated oven at 400°F/200°C/Gas 6 for 10–12 minutes until golden.

Soufflé SPECIAL

The special thing about this soufflé is that firstly, it doesn't collapse like classic soufflés when you bring it to the table, and secondly, it goes substantially further so that it is almost a meal in itself. Lovely with salads if your children like them, or with leeks in the winter, courgettes in the summer.

FOR 4

1 onion, chopped
1 tablespoon olive oil
125 g (4 oz) leftover vegetables (mushrooms, peas, leeks, sweetcorn, broccoli etc), chopped where necessary
125 g (4 oz) pasta shapes, cooked 'al dente'

175 ml (6 fl. oz) béchamel (see page 14)
75 g (3 oz) mature Cheddar cheese, grated
2 eggs, separated
1 tablespoon grated Parmesan cheese

Soften the onion in the oil and stir in the chopped vegetables of your choice. Stir until well mixed together, and then mix with the pasta shapes. Stir in the béchamel and the Cheddar cheese thoroughly. Beat the yolks and mix in. Whisk the whites until very stiff and fold in. Place in a greased soufflé dish and sprinkle with Parmesan. Bake in a preheated oven at 375°F/190°C/Gas 5 for 15–20 minutes until well risen and set. Serve immediately.

GOOEY OMELETTE ★

Eating this concoction can be quite a game since you can wrap the Gruyère seemingly endlessly around the fork just like spaghetti! It makes a quick and delicious meal, best served with potatoes and a crisp salad or side vegetables.

FOR 4

175 g (6 oz) spaghetti, cooked and chopped into 2.5 cm (1 inch) lengths

75 g (3 oz) Gruyère cheese, grated finely

salt and pepper

5 eggs, beaten with 4 tablespoons milk

25 g (1 oz) butter

Mix the warm, chopped spaghetti with the Gruyère and season with black pepper and a little salt. Make the omelette in the usual way, with the butter, using a very big pan (or use half of the mixture at a time and make two omelettes). As the omelette begins to set and cook through, place the spaghetti filling on top of it. Fold it in half, continue cooking, and when it is done through cut into four wedges and serve at once.

PETE'S PASTA ★

The joy of this pasta dish is that you can prepare it well in advance, and pop it into the oven – a nutritious meal in itself – less than 30 minutes before you want to eat. The crunchy topping is irresistible and makes an original finishing touch.

FOR 4

125 g (4 oz) mushrooms, sliced

2 tablespoons vegetable oil

300 g (10 oz) pasta shapes, cooked '*al dente*'

250 g (8 oz) cottage cheese

125 g (4 oz) low-fat cream cheese

1 medium onion, finely chopped

1 tablespoon mixed dried herbs

salt and pepper

2 tablespoons each ground roasted peanuts and sesame seeds

50 g (2 oz) Cheddar cheese, grated

Sauté the mushrooms in the hot oil very quickly so that they are cooked but still crisp. Mix into the cooked pasta shapes. Liquidize the cottage cheese to a purée with the cream cheese and mix in the onion and herbs. Season with salt and pepper and toss this mixture into the pasta. Combine the peanuts, sesame seeds and grated cheese and top the dish with this mixture. Bake in a preheated oven at 350°F/180°C/Gas 4 for 20 minutes.

NOODLE DOODLE

This is a beautifully convenient way of putting virtually all the ingredients that you need for a meal into one dish. It sets like a savoury custard, and makes soft and satisfying food.

FOR 4

125 g (4 oz) thin noodles, cooked '*al dente*'
125 g (4 oz) mushrooms, quartered and sautéed in a little oil
2 leeks, cooked and chopped

2 tablespoons olive oil
salt and pepper
4 eggs
300 ml ($\frac{1}{2}$ pint) stock (see page 13)

Mix the noodles with the prepared vegetables and moisten with the olive oil. Season to taste with salt and pepper. Beat the eggs and stir in the stock. Pour this over the noodle mixture and cover with foil. Stand in a tray of hot water and bake in a preheated oven at 325°F/160°C/Gas 3 for 35–40 minutes, until set. Leave to stand for 5 minutes before serving.

BEST CHEESE PIE

I have been making this for my young family for years and they never seem to tire of it. Rather the reverse – it is frequently on the request list, and I never have any leftovers because it is as good cold as it is hot.

FOR 4

150 ml (¼ pint) béchamel (see page 14)
50 g (2 oz) Gruyère cheese, grated
25 g (1 oz) Cheddar cheese, grated
salt, pepper and grated nutmeg
2 eggs, separated

1 × 20 cm (8 inch) shortcrust pastry case, baked blind (or use the potato pastry on page 13)
1 tablespoon grated Parmesan cheese

Heat the béchamel gently and stir in the Gruyère and Cheddar until they melt. Season to taste with salt, pepper and nutmeg and remove from the heat. Beat the egg yolks thoroughly and stir into the cheese mixture. Whisk the whites until very stiff and fold in quickly, and then pour into the prepared pastry shell. Sprinkle with Parmesan, and bake in a preheated oven at 400°F/200°C/Gas 6 for 12–15 minutes, until puffed and set. Serve immediately.

BEST CHEESE PUDDING

This, like the cheese pie above, is a winner with my family and friends. The lining of sliced bread crisps up to become golden and crunchy, whilst the inside is light, cheesy and tasty. Delicious with any of the fruit and vegetable salads on pages 67–68.

FOR 4

4 large slices bread
margarine or butter
2 eggs, beaten
150 ml (¼ pint) milk

250 g (8 oz) Cheddar or Edam cheese, diced
½ teaspoon dry mustard powder
salt and pepper

Spread the bread with the margarine or butter and cut each slice into 8 strips. Put a layer on to the bottom of a greased baking dish. Arrange the rest of the strips upright around the sides. Mix the eggs with the milk, cheese and mustard, and season to taste. Bake in a preheated oven at 350°F/180°C/Gas 4 for 30 minutes.

Scone Pizza ★

Much as I enjoy making pizzas with the classic yeast dough, I am eternally grateful to the friend who generously gave me this recipe. It is so simple and quick to prepare, and the plain scone-like mixture makes a scrumptious base for this tasty topping.

FOR 4

FOR THE BASE
125 g (4 oz) self-raising flour
½ teaspoon salt
1 teaspoon dried herbs
25 g (1 oz) margarine
2 tablespoons each milk and water

FOR THE TOPPING
2 large onions, sliced
3 tablespoons vegetable oil
50 g (2 oz) mushrooms, sliced
salt and pepper
3 tomatoes, sliced
50 g (2 oz) mature Cheddar cheese, grated

For the base, sift the flour with the salt and mix in the herbs. Rub in the margarine and then mix to a dough with the milk and water. Press down into an oiled 20 cm (8 inch) flan tin.

For the topping, soften the onion in the oil, covered, over a gentle heat for 10 minutes, stirring from time to time. Stir in the mushrooms and cook through. Season with a little salt and pepper and put on top of the scone base. Cover with slices of tomato and finish with the grated cheese. Bake in a preheated oven at 400°F/200°C/Gas 6 for 30 minutes.

TOMATO CHARLOTTE ★

Crisply baked, the slices of bread turn golden, and inside there is a soft filling of more bread and tomatoes, highlighted by herbs. The cheese on top, browned and bubbly, completes this wonderful dish.

FOR 4

6 thin slices bread
75 g (3 oz) margarine or butter
1 × 14 oz (400 g) can tomatoes,
   drained and sliced
salt and pepper

a small bunch of fresh herbs such as
   basil, chopped, *or* 2 tablespoons
   mixed dried herbs
50 g (2 oz) Cheddar cheese, grated

Butter the slices of bread and slice each one into three fingers. Line a small oiled soufflé dish around the edges and on the bottom with some of these bread slices, buttered side under and out. Put in a layer of tomatoes, season with salt and pepper and sprinkle on some herbs. Cover with more bread slices and repeat the layers until the bread is used up. Finish with a layer of grated cheese and bake in a preheated oven at 350°F/180°C/Gas 4 for 30 minutes.

CRISPY PLATE PANCAKES

This is a novel way of making pancakes, which is rather like a pizza base. In this recipe they are topped with gently fried eggs and herbs, but you can also use them as a base for any mixture of vegetables or mushrooms, creamed or stir-fried.

FOR 4

150 g (5 oz) plain flour, sifted
salt and pepper
2 large eggs, separated
300 ml (½ pint) milk
25 g (1 oz) Parmesan cheese, grated

vegetable oil
4 eggs
25 g (1 oz) butter or margarine
2 tablespoons fresh mixed herbs,
   chopped

Liquidize the flour, a pinch of salt, egg yolks, milk, Parmesan and 1 teaspoon oil to a thick batter. Leave to stand for a couple of hours, then fold in the stiffly beaten egg whites. Cook in a lightly greased, heavy frying pan in 15 cm (6 inch) rounds in hot oil until the pancakes are crisp and puffed, and golden on both sides. Make four pancakes, and keep warm.

Fry the four eggs gently in a little butter or margarine until set. Season with salt and pepper and sprinkle with herbs. Place each one on to a pancake and serve immediately.

MUSHROOM COBBLER ★

Baking mushrooms in this way brings out the best in their flavour – nothing is added except for a little flavouring, and they are cooked lightly without spoiling their delicacy. The light and cheesy cobbler topping is delicious dipped into their juices.

FOR 4

FOR THE TOPPING
75 g (3 oz) each wholewheat and plain
   flour
2 teaspoons baking powder
½ teaspoon salt
75 g (3 oz) Cheddar cheese, grated
1 egg, beaten
60 ml (2 fl oz) milk
1 tablespoon olive oil
1 tablespoon sesame seeds

FOR THE FILLING
350 g (12 oz) flat mushrooms
salt and pepper

For the topping, sift the flours with the baking powder and salt, and mix in the cheese. Fold in the beaten egg and then mix to a dough with the milk and oil. Knead until smooth on a floured board, then roll out to a 20 cm (8 inch) circle about 1 cm (½ inch) thick and sprinkle with the sesame seeds.

Place the mushrooms, whole, in a round 20 cm (8 inch) dish, and season with salt and pepper before pressing down lightly. Place the cobbler circle on top of them and bake in a preheated oven at 400°F/200°C/Gas 6 for 25 minutes.

Stuffed Baked Potatoes ★

There is something immensely satisfying about a baked potato as the central feature of a meal. They always smell wonderful while they are cooking, and the three separate fillings here make a mouth-watering meal out of very basic ingredients simply mixed together.

FOR 6

6 large potatoes, scrubbed
grated cheese, to sprinkle

FILLING 1
125 g (4 oz) sweetcorn
125 g (4 oz) cooked spinach, chopped
50 g (2 oz) Cheddar cheese, grated
25 g (1 oz) butter, softened
salt and pepper

FILLING 2

125 g (4 oz) peas, cooked
1 lettuce, finely shredded and
  blanched
1 small avocado, its flesh mashed
50 g (2 oz) Edam cheese, grated
salt and pepper

FILLING 3

300 ml ($\frac{1}{2}$ pint) béchamel (see page 14)
250 g (8 oz) mushrooms, sliced and
  sautéed in a little oil or butter

Bake the potatoes in their skins in a preheated oven at 400°F/200°C/Gas 6 for 1¼ hours. Cut them lengthwise and scoop out the flesh. Mix half of this with the prepared stuffing of your choice and heap back into the skins. Sprinkle with grated cheese and put back into the oven for a further 20 minutes to heat through. You can use the leftover potato flesh for making the potato pastry on page 13, in the Crusty Broccoli and Mushroom Bake (see page 50), or for the Gâteau di Patate on page 37.

ELEGANT EGG FLAN

This unusual flan, with its crunchy base, always wins cries of '*encore*' in my family. It is equally wonderful hot, warm or cold, and is best, in my opinion, served with a variety of salads.

FOR 4

FOR THE FLAN CRUST
50 g (2 oz) dried breadcrumbs
50 g (2 oz) wholewheat flour
50 g (2 oz) oat flakes
15 g ($\frac{1}{2}$ oz) sesame seeds, toasted
75 g (3 oz) butter or margarine, melted

FOR THE FILLING
175 g (6 oz) cabbage, shredded finely
3 tablespoons vegetable oil
125 g (4 oz) mushrooms, sliced
salt and pepper
50 g (2 oz) butter or margarine
4 eggs

For the flan crust, mix the breadcrumbs, flour, oat flakes and sesame seeds and stir into the melted fat. Mix thoroughly until well amalgamated and press into a well oiled 20 cm (8 inch) flan tin. Bake in a preheated oven at 375°F/190°C/Gas 5 for 15–20 minutes. Cool.

For the filling, sauté the shredded cabbage in the oil until it is cooked but still crunchy. Add the mushrooms and cook them so that they are also cooked but still crisp. Season with salt and pepper, remove from the pan and keep warm. Melt the butter or margarine and break the eggs into the pan. Whisk with a fork or wire whisk and season with salt and pepper. Cook over a moderate heat and as the eggs begin to scramble, add the mushroom and cabbage mixture. Be careful not to overcook the eggs – they should be moist and creamy, not dry. Pile into the cooked pie crust. Serve hot, warm or cold. If you wish, you can use the Crispy Pastry with sesame seeds for the base (see page 13).

ROSEMARY'S RISOTTO

I love risottos: there are so many variations on the theme and quite often the best ones are made with whatever happens to be in the fridge at the time. This one, with leeks, tomatoes and two different sorts of cheese, is one of my favourites.

FOR 4

1 large onion, chopped
3 tablespoons olive oil
175 g (6 oz) long-grain rice, washed
  and drained
2 large leeks, cooked and finely sliced

3 large tomatoes, skinned and
  chopped
salt, pepper and mixed dried herbs
50 g (2 oz) Emmental cheese, cubed
grated Parmesan cheese

Cook the onion gently in the olive oil until it is soft, and then add the rice, stirring thoroughly so that the grains become coated with oil. Add water to cover, and cook gently until it is absorbed by the rice, stirring occasionally. Then add more water and continue cooking in this way until the rice is tender. Just before it is completely cooked, add the leeks and tomatoes and season with salt, pepper and mixed dried herbs. When the rice is done, toss in the cheese cubes and allow to heat through so that they begin to melt. Serve each helping with a sprinkling of Parmesan.

CHEESE TRIANGLES

This must be my most worn recipe card! The kids love these light, golden puff-pastry packets filled with hot creamy cheese with its tang of herbs and onion. They look pretty sensational, too – you should have no shortage of converts on your hands!

FOR 4

1 × 500 g (1 lb) packet puff pastry
75 g (3 oz) low-fat cream cheese
175 g (6 oz) Cheddar cheese, finely
  grated

1 small onion, finely chopped
2 egg yolks
salt, pepper and dried mixed herbs

Roll the pastry out thinly on a floured board and cut it into eight 10 cm (4 inch) squares. Blend the cream cheese with the Cheddar, onion and one of the egg yolks, beaten. Season with salt, pepper and dried herbs. Heap some of the mixture on to the centre of each pastry square and fold over to form a triangle, sealing very thoroughly by moistening the inner edges with water and pressing together with a fork. Brush with the remaining beaten egg yolk and place on a well-greased baking tray. Cook in a preheated oven at 425°F/220°C/Gas 7 for 15 minutes.

GÂTEAU DI PATATE

This recipe was given to me by an Italian friend who always produced · marvellous meals. It soon became a stand-by in my family, and you can vary the vegetables that go into it to suit your family's taste: the sweetcorn and peas here being the simplest possible variation.

FOR 4–6

1 kg (2 lb) potatoes, peeled and cooked	1 large garlic clove, crushed (optional)
25 g (1 oz) butter or margarine	1 × 200 g (7 oz) can sweetcorn, drained
4–5 tablespoons milk	125 g (4 oz) peas, cooked
300 ml ($\frac{1}{2}$ pint) double cream	2 tablespoons grated Parmesan cheese
75 g (3 oz) Jarlsberg cheese, finely diced	

Mash the potatoes thoroughly with the butter or margarine and the milk – they should be quite stiff and dry. Make a border with two-thirds of them around the edge of a large, oiled, oval serving dish. Whip the cream until thick and fold in the diced cheese, garlic (if used), sweetcorn and peas. Place this mixture in the centre of the dish. Cover with a layer of the remaining potatoes, sprinkle with Parmesan, and cook in a preheated oven at 400°F/200°C/Gas 6 for 45 minutes.

SUPER SUPPER SLICE ★

All very simple and homely, this loaf is satisfying, nourishing food – some might call it nursery food – but delicious and popular for all that. It's the kind of recipe that fast becomes a stand-by in a vegetarian family.

FOR 4

2 onions, finely chopped	2 tablespoons mixed dried herbs
50 g (2 oz) margarine	2 teaspoons yeast extract
50 g (2 oz) rolled oats	2 eggs, separated
175 g (6 oz) cheese, grated	salt and pepper

Soften the onion in the margarine over a gentle heat, and then stir in the oats. Mix until well coated. Add the cheese, herbs and yeast extract and mix well. Stir in the beaten egg yolks and season to taste with salt and pepper. Fold in the stiffly beaten egg whites and cook in a preheated oven at 375°F/190°C/ Gas 5 for about 25 minutes until set. Allow to cool in the tin for 10 minutes or so before turning out. Serve sliced, warm or cold.

PUFFY SOUFFLÉ

This dish is virtually a meal in itself – beautifully filling and satisfying – and mouth-watering smells come from the oven whilst it is cooking. Serve it with your childrens' favourite vegetables and you will be popular!

FOR 4

450 ml (¾ pint) milk	1 garlic clove, crushed (optional)
125 g (4 oz) dried breadcrumbs	salt and pepper
150 g (5 oz) Cheddar cheese, grated	150 g (5 oz) canned sweetcorn, drained
25 g (1 oz) butter or margarine	3 eggs, separated

Bring the milk to boiling point. Stir in the crumbs and add 125 g (4 oz) of the cheese, the butter or margarine and the garlic (if used). Season to taste and stir in the sweetcorn. Cool a little and stir in the beaten egg yolks. Then fold in the stiffly beaten egg whites and pour into a well greased 25 cm (10 inch) soufflé dish. Sprinkle with the rest of the cheese and bake in a preheated oven at 375°F/190°C/Gas 5 for 30–35 minutes until risen and golden. Serve immediately.

Vegemites' Spaghetti

I have made this dish so many times for my kids and their friends that I have lost count of the number. All I can remember is that each time I cook it they love it, and there is never any left at the end of the meal!

FOR 4

3 large onions, sliced
3 tablespoons oil
1 × 400 g (14 oz) can tomatoes,
    drained and chopped
2 tablespoons mixed dried herbs

salt and pepper
125 g (4 oz) Cheddar cheese, grated
250 g (8 oz) spaghetti, cooked
extra grated cheese, to sprinkle

Soften the onions in the oil over a very gentle heat, covered, stirring occasionally, for 15–20 minutes, by which time they should be translucent and slightly sweet. Stir in the tomatoes and mix well, and then add the herbs and season to taste with salt and pepper. Finally stir in the Cheddar until it melts. Liquidize the mixture and toss into the hot drained spaghetti. Sprinkle extra cheese over each portion.

GREEDY GREEN SLICES

These are a cunning way to get kids to start eating pulses. The lentils and mung beans are the mainstay of the slices but are subtly disguised by the way in which they are cooked. I have found the most conservative of children wolfing them down!

FOR 6

125 g (4 oz) green lentils, soaked for 2 hours
125 g (4 oz) mung beans, soaked for 2 hours
2 bay leaves
salt and pepper

1 large onion, chopped
125 g (4 oz) Cheddar cheese, grated
150 ml (¼ pint) stock
2 eggs, beaten
2 tablespoons mixed dried herbs

Drain the soaked lentils and mung beans and put in a saucepan with the bay leaves. Boil until tender, about 20 minutes. Drain, and season with salt. Alternatively, if you are in a hurry substitute baked beans for the other pulses.

Mix in the onion, cheese, stock and well beaten eggs. Season with the herbs, and more salt and pepper to taste. Put into a 500 g (1 lb) loaf tin and bake in a preheated oven at 350°F/180°C/Gas 4 for 1 hour. Allow to cool in the tin for 10–15 minutes, then turn out and serve in slices.

SHEPHERDESS CRUMBLE ★

The utterly delectable crunchy topping to the dish is no mean substitute for the carnivore's Shepherd's Pie. I personally think that it is streets ahead of a boring mixture of mince and potatoes . . .

FOR 4–6

1 large onion, chopped
3 tablespoons oil
75 g (3 oz) mushrooms, sliced
125 g (4 oz) black-eyed beans, cooked
   (or baked beans if you're in a hurry)
2 medium leeks, cooked and sliced
125 g (4 oz) French beans or
   courgettes, cooked and chopped
salt and pepper
garlic to taste, crushed (optional)

FOR THE CRUMBLE

75 g (3 oz) oat or barley flakes
50 g (2 oz) wholewheat flour, sifted
   with 1 teaspoon baking powder
2 tablespoons sunflower seeds
2 tablespoons walnuts finely chopped
75 g (3 oz) butter or margarine, melted

Soften the onion in the oil over a gentle heat until soft, for about 10 minutes, when it will be translucent and slightly sweet. Stir in the mushrooms and cook, stirring, until they begin to soften. Stir in the beans, leeks and green vegetables. Mix well, and season to taste with salt, pepper and garlic (if used). Place in a well-greased soufflé dish.

For the crumble, mix the dry ingredients together and stir thoroughly into the melted fat. Season with salt and pepper and sprinkle over the top of the vegetables. Bake in a preheated oven at 350°F/180°C/Gas 4 for 20–25 minutes.

VERY GOOD
VEGETABLES

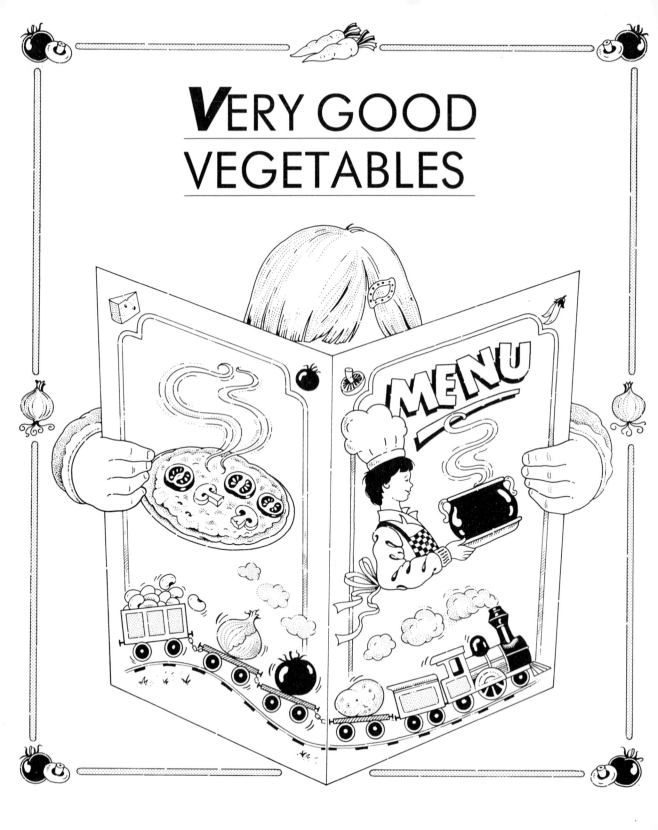

These vegetable recipes are a far cry from dreary supplements to a main course. Some of them are delicious just on their own with a salad, and others are new and mouth-watering ways of treating the everyday side vegetable which will keep the kids ever-enthusiastic!

OATMEAL TOMATOES

A crisp coating of oatmeal, fried until browned, makes these slices of tomato utterly irresistible. When fresh tomatoes are at their height in the summer I use this recipe frequently, and we never tire of it.

FOR 4–6

500 g (1 lb) tomatoes, sliced
salt and pepper

75 g (3 oz) medium oatmeal
5 tablespoons vegetable oil

Season the sliced tomatoes with salt and pepper and dip them in the oatmeal so that they are covered all over. Fry in hot vegetable oil until browned and crisp on both sides, then drain on kitchen paper and keep warm until ready to serve.

CUNNING CARROTS ★

My kids love this way of cooking carrots – it makes a welcome change from just boiling or steaming them, and brings out their sweetness. Lovely with the Cheese Pie on page 30.

FOR 4

350 g (12 oz) carrots, grated
2 tablespoons dried herbs

salt and pepper
50 g (2 oz) butter or margarine, melted

Mix the grated carrots with the herbs, and season with salt and pepper. Toss in the melted butter or margarine and put in a heatproof dish under a medium grill. Cook until a crust forms, about 8–10 minutes.

CARROTS IN FOIL ★

This recipe has two major virtues: one is how easy it is for the cook, the other is the way that the carrots retain their fresh and wholesome taste. A delicious dish for all times of the year.

FOR 4

350 g (12 oz) baby carrots   25 g (1 oz) butter or margarine
salt and pepper

Simply sprinkle the carrots with a little salt and pepper and dot them with butter or margarine. Wrap them up in a foil parcel and bake in a preheated oven at 350°F/180°C/Gas 4 for 30 minutes.

CHEESY POTATO CROQUETTES

These crisp, cheesy croquettes make a really special side vegetable to go with a simple main course, and are also a delicious supper dish in their own right, served with salads of your choice.

FOR 4–6

500 g (1 lb) potatoes, peeled, cooked and mashed
1 × 350 g (12 oz) carton cottage cheese, puréed in the blender
50 g (2 oz) peanuts, ground coarsely
6 spring onions, finely sliced

50 g (2 oz) Cheddar cheese, finely grated
salt, pepper and grated nutmeg
2 egg yolks, beaten
4 tablespoons dried breadcrumbs
150 ml ($\frac{1}{4}$ pint) vegetable oil

Combine the mashed potatoes with the puréed cottage cheese, peanuts, spring onions and Cheddar. Mix very thoroughly, season to taste with salt, pepper and nutmeg, and stir in the egg yolks to bind the mixture. Form into croquettes and roll in breadcrumbs. Chill. Fry in hot vegetable oil, turning until golden all over. Drain on kitchen paper and keep in a warm oven until ready to serve.

VEGETABLES IN PARCELS

This method of deep-frying vegetables wrapped up in rice paper was a revelation to me when I first tried it out, and once discovered I couldn't leave it alone! The paper crisps up, and the vegetables inside are lightly cooked through, retaining the best of their flavour.

350 g (12 oz) cauliflower or broccoli, cut into florets, *or*
350 g (12 oz) courgettes, carrots or leeks, sliced 1 cm (½ inch) thick, *or*

250 g (8 oz) small button mushrooms
rice paper
vegetable oil for deep frying

Wrap the vegetable in a little square of rice paper, making sure that the parcel is securely sealed by moistening the free edges down. Fry in very hot oil (425°F/220°C) for a few minutes until the paper is crisp, turning from time to time. Drain on kitchen paper and keep hot. Serve as soon as possible.

CORN FRITTERS

These are disgustingly delicious and totally more-ish. In my house they disappear as fast as I create them, and I can never cook enough of them. Delicious as a light meal on their own with salads, they are also an excellent accompaniment to the Mushroom Loaf on Page 24.

FOR 4

3 eggs, separated
50 g (2 oz) wholewheat flour
1 × 300 g (11 oz) can sweetcorn, drained

salt and pepper
5 tablespoons vegetable oil

Beat the egg yolks and stir in the flour. Beat again. Stir in the sweetcorn and season to taste. Beat the egg whites until very stiff, and fold in. Heat the oil in a heavy pan and fry the mixture in rounds of about 7 cm (3 inches) in diameter. Give them about 2 minutes on each side so that they are crisp and golden all over.

SESAME POTATO CAKES ★

The delicate flavour of sesame marries well with potatoes, and these little cakes are something slightly different to go with a simple main course like the Gooey Omelette on page 28.

FOR 4

500 g (1 lb) potatoes, peeled and
   cooked
40 g (1½ oz) margarine or butter
2–3 tablespoons milk

50 g (2 oz) sesame seeds
1 egg yolk, beaten
salt and pepper
5 tablespoons sesame oil

Mash the potatoes with the margarine or butter, and milk. Grill 40 g (1½ oz) of the sesame seeds until browned and stir in with the egg yolk to thoroughly bind the mixture. Season with salt and pepper and mix to a firm consistency. Shape into 5 cm (2 inch) rounds about 1 cm (½ inch) thick, and dip in the remaining sesame seeds. Fry gently in the sesame oil until golden, about 5 minutes on each side. Drain on kitchen paper and keep hot until ready to serve.

MUSHROOM MUNCH

This is a sensational way of combining mushrooms and potatoes in a side vegetable dish, which you can put in the oven and then forget about for an hour. The potatoes are sliced paper thin, and cook rather like the potatoes in a gratin dauphinois, with the mushrooms making a tasty layer on top.

FOR 4

125 g (4 oz) mushrooms, sliced
450 ml (¾ pint) béchamel (see page 14)

500 g (1 lb) potatoes, peeled and sliced
   very thinly
salt and pepper

Add the sliced mushrooms to the béchamel and mix well. Rinse the sliced potatoes, dry them on a cloth, and put into a greased ovenproof dish. Season with salt and pepper. Pour the mushroom mixture over the potatoes and bake in a preheated oven at 350°F/180°C/Gas 4 for 1 hour.

TEMPTING CABBAGE

Although this takes time and care to prepare, your efforts will be rewarded – it is a truly memorable way of dealing with cabbage and makes an excellent course all on its own – a meal in itself.

FOR 4–6

1 medium cabbage	**50 g (2 oz) butter, melted**
50 g (2 oz) oatmeal	**1 egg yolk, beaten**
1 small onion, chopped	**450 ml ($\frac{3}{4}$ pint) béchamel (see page 14)**
3 teaspoons mixed dried herbs	**salt and pepper**
50 g (2 oz) mushrooms, chopped	**25 g (1 oz) dried breadcrumbs**
25 g (1 oz) Parmesan cheese, grated	**75 g (3 oz) Cheddar cheese, grated**

Remove about 12 of the best outer cabbage leaves whole, and blanch them in boiling water for 3–4 minutes. Drain and cool.

Combine the oatmeal with the onion, herbs, mushrooms and Parmesan, and toss into the melted butter. Mix very thoroughly and then stir in the beaten egg yolk. Shred the remaining inner cabbage finely, mix with 150 ml ($\frac{1}{4}$ pint) of the béchamel, and season to taste. Line the bottom of a well greased ovenproof dish with this mixture.

Place spoonfuls of the oatmeal stuffing into the outer cabbage leaves and roll up into little parcels. Place over the top of the creamed cabbage and cover with the remaining béchamel. Mix the dried breadcrumbs with the Cheddar and sprinkle over the top. Bake in a preheated oven at 375°F/190°C/Gas 5 for 25–30 minutes.

GRATED POTATO HASH ★

Cooking grated potatoes very slowly and gently preserves the marvellous subtle taste which often gets lost when they are boiled. This is one of my most favourite ways of eating potatoes, and is delicious with simple omelettes or quiches.

500 g (1 lb) potatoes, peeled and grated

50 g (2 oz) butter or margarine
salt, pepper and grated nutmeg

Soak the grated potato in cold water, then drain and dry on a towel. Melt the butter in a heavy pan and stir in the potato over a moderate heat, turning until well coated in the butter. As the potato begins to soften, season with salt, pepper and nutmeg, and then turn the heat right down. Press the potatoes down to make a kind of cake, and cover wih a lid or with foil. Cook for about 45 minutes or until well browned underneath. Turn out onto a hot platter, brown side up, to serve.

GREEN GRATIN ★

Mung beans and cheese go wonderfully well together, and this gratin is an excellent way of introducing kids to pulses, and convincing them – if they need convincing – of how delicious they are.

FOR 4–6

125 g (4 oz) mung beans, soaked for 1 hour
1 bay leaf
1 small onion, peeled and cut in half

175 g (6 oz) peas, cooked
300 ml ($\frac{1}{2}$ pint) béchamel (see page 14)
salt and pepper
50 g (2 oz) Cheddar cheese, grated

Drain the soaked mung beans and put into a saucepan with water to cover. Add the bay leaf and onion halves and simmer for 15–20 minutes until cooked. Drain, and remove the bay leaf and onion. Combine the mung beans with the peas and mix into the béchamel. Season to taste with salt and pepper and put into an ovenproof dish. Cover with the grated cheese and bake in a preheated oven at 350°F/180°C/Gas 4 for 10–15 minutes.

FLAGEOLET AND MUSHROOM GRATIN

I think that flageolets are amongst the most delicious of the pulses, and combined with mushrooms in a cheesy sauce they make a mouth-watering side vegetable.

FOR 4–6

250 g (8 oz) flageolets, soaked and
   cooked (see page 12)
salt, pepper and mixed dried herbs
1 garlic clove, crushed (optional)
250 g (8 oz) small button mushrooms,
   quartered

300 ml ($\frac{1}{2}$ pint) béchamel (see page 14)
40 g ($1\frac{1}{2}$ oz) Cheddar cheese, finely
   grated
25 g (1 oz) dried breadcrumbs

Season the flageolets with salt, pepper and mixed dried herbs, and the garlic (if used). Place in the bottom of a well-greased ovenproof dish. Mix the mushrooms into the béchamel and heat through until they begin to give their flavour to the sauce. Season to taste and pour over the flageolets. Mix together the cheese and breadcrumbs and cover the dish with this mixture. Bake in a preheated oven at 350°F/180°C/Gas 4 for 15–20 minutes.

TOP TOMATOES ★

Layers of tomatoes, breadcrumbs and mushrooms make an excellent side vegetable, baked with a cheesy finish, to go with any main course. I have yet to have leftovers of this dish!

FOR 4

4 medium tomatoes, skinned and
   sliced
50 g (2 oz) breadcrumbs

125 g (4 oz) mushrooms, sliced
125 g (4 oz) Cheddar cheese, grated
salt and pepper

Grease a small ovenproof dish. Make layers with the tomatoes, breadcrumbs, mushrooms and cheese, seasoning the vegetable layers as you go. Finish with a cheese layer, and bake in a preheated oven at 350°F/180°C/Gas 4 for 30 minutes.

LENTIL STIRABOUT

Mixing lentils with other appetizing ingredients is a good way to get kids to like them, if you have any problems. Conservative creatures that children are, the poor old lentil always needs a bit of disguise. This works!

FOR 6–8

125 g (4 oz) mushrooms, sliced
2 tablespoons olive oil
175 g (6 oz) lentils, cooked
175 g (6 oz) noodles, cooked
125 g (4 oz) tiny cauliflower florets,
   steamed

50 g (2 oz) Cheddar cheese, grated
2 tablespoons grated Parmesan cheese
salt and pepper

Cook the sliced mushrooms in the olive oil until soft. Mix with the lentils, noodles and cauliflower florets, and stir in the cheese. Heat through over a gentle heat, stirring, and then put into a heatproof dish. Sprinkle with the Parmesan and brown under a hot grill for a minute or two.

CRUSTY BROCCOLI AND MUSHROOM BAKE

A nutty oatmeal topping gives a delectable crunch to this mixture of creamed broccoli and mushrooms, and for many kids it is a more acceptable way of eating vegetables than in their plain state, steamed or boiled.

FOR 4–6

125 g (4 oz) mushrooms, sliced
450 ml ($\frac{3}{4}$ pint) béchamel (see page 14)
300 g (10 oz) broccoli florets, lightly
   steamed

75 g (3 oz) medium oatmeal
50 g (2 oz) walnuts, chopped
75 g (3 oz) Cheddar cheese, grated
salt and pepper

Mix the mushrooms into the béchamel and heat through gently. Season to taste. Pour this over the broccoli in an ovenproof dish. Mix together the oatmeal, walnuts and Cheddar and sprinkle over the top. Bake in a preheated oven at 375°F/190°C/Gas 5 for 12–15 minutes.

NUTTY CABBAGE ★

If you have any problems getting your kids to eat their greens, try this on them – just once should be enough! It has a high conversion rate.

FOR 4–6

1 medium cabbage, finely shredded
75 g (3 oz) dry-roasted peanuts, coarsely ground
1 small onion, thinly sliced and chopped

4 tablespoons vegetable oil
sea salt and pepper

Mix the cabbage, nuts and onion together. Heat the oil and stir-fry for 8–10 minutes until the cabbage is cooked and hot, but still crisp. Season to taste, and it is ready to serve.

CRUNCHY POTATOES ★

This is an easy way of making potato cakes, and cuts out the slightly messy business of frying them in oil.

FOR 4–6

500 g (1 lb) potatoes, peeled, boiled and mashed
5 tablespoons mayonnaise (see page 14)

1 egg, beaten
50 g (2 oz) barley flakes

Mash the mayonnaise into the potatoes and roll into twelve balls. Roll in the beaten egg and then the crushed barley flakes. Bake in a preheated oven at 375°F/190°C/Gas 5 for 15–20 minutes.

GRATED POTATO PANCAKES

Browned and crispy, tasty and aromatic, these little pancakes are hopelessly irresistible. They make a treat of a meal, and I often use them as a side vegetable for Sunday lunch as something rather special.

FOR 4

4 medium potatoes, peeled and grated
1 small onion, finely chopped
2 tablespoons wholewheat flour

2 eggs, beaten
salt and pepper
vegetable oil for frying

Rinse the grated potatoes to wash off the starch, and dry them on a towel. Mix in the onion and the flour, and stir in the beaten eggs. Mix thoroughly and season with salt and pepper. Drop spoonfuls into hot oil in a shallow frying pan and cook for about 5 minutes on each side until they are crisp and golden. Drain on kitchen paper and serve as hot as possible.

CHEESY ROAST POTATOES

If I had to choose any one way of cooking potatoes this would have to be the winner: very crisply roasted, browned potatoes moistened with cheese which also finishes up crisp, making an unbeatable side vegetable.

FOR 4

1 kg (2 lb) medium potatoes, peeled
5 tablespoons vegetable oil
salt and pepper

75 g (3 oz) Cheddar cheese, finely
    grated

Cut into the potatoes with a sharp knife, making thin slices to about three-quarters of the way through, leaving the bottom uncut. Place in a baking tray and trickle the oil over them. Season with salt and pepper. Roast at 325°F/160°C/Gas 3 for 2 hours, basting periodically. Sprinkle the grated cheese over the top after the first hour of cooking.

*F*AST
FUN FOOD

The image of fast food is that it is junk food. This section proves that you need not be a slave to the stove in order to feed your kids healthily, but rather you will find that you can give them simple, quick, nutritious meals which smell and taste wonderful – and all in a matter of minutes.

Tomatoes with eggs ★

When you get hold of those really large 'beef' tomatoes (as they are so unsuitably called), this is a delightful way of dealing with them. The filling of herbed cheese, all melted, and topped with a baked egg, makes each one an individual meal in itself, placed on toast or (my personal favourite vice) fried bread.

FOR 4

2 large beef tomatoes, cut in half	sea salt and black pepper
125 g (4 oz) cheese, grated	4 eggs
1 medium bunch parsley, finely chopped	2 tablespoons dried breadcrumbs
	2 tablespoons grated Parmesan cheese
4 tablespoons olive oil	4 slices toast or fried bread

Scoop the flesh out of the tomatoes and discard the woody centres. Mix the soft flesh with the cheese, parsley and olive oil and season to taste. Put the mixture in to the bottom of the hollow tomato shells and bake for 10 minutes in a preheated oven at 350°F/180°C/Gas 4. Then break an egg into each one, cover with the breadcrumbs and Parmesan mixed together, and bake for a further 5–7 minutes until the eggs are lightly set. Place each tomato on a piece of fried bread or toast and serve at once.

Nutty rarebit ★

The simple device of a few chopped peanuts added to a Welsh Rarebit mixture makes a crunchy and delicious snack piled on to hot buttered toast. Use wholemeal bread, and this little meal has a perfect nutritional balance.

FOR 2–3

3 tablespoons milk	50 g (2 oz) dry-roasted peanuts
25 g (1oz) margarine or butter	salt and pepper
125 g (4 oz) Cheddar cheese, grated	1 egg, beaten
1 teaspoon dry mustard powder	2–3 slices wholemeal bread, toasted

Put the milk, margarine or butter and grated cheese into a heavy saucepan and stir over a low heat until the cheese melts and the mixture turns creamy. Add the mustard, then stir in the peanuts and season to taste. Fold in the beaten egg and put on to slices of toast in a heatproof dish. Place under a hot grill for a few moments until it begins to turn golden. Serve at once.

Swiss bliss ★

The Swiss are renowned for their fabulous cheese dishes – a simple fondue made with Gruyère is an unforgettable experience. Their cookery tends to be pretty rich, as this dish is, but it is lovely on really cold days for really hungry people.

FOR 4

15 g ($\frac{1}{2}$ oz) margarine or butter, softened	4 eggs
	salt, pepper and grated nutmeg
125 g (4 oz) Gruyère cheese, very thinly sliced	150 ml ($\frac{1}{4}$ pint) thick set yogurt

Spread the softened margarine or butter over the bottom of a heatproof dish and cover with half of the cheese slices. Break the eggs on top, and season well with salt, pepper and nutmeg. Spoon over the yogurt, and cover with the remaining cheese slices. Bake in a preheated oven at 400°F/200°C/Gas 6 for 5–8 minutes until the eggs are lightly set, then put under a very hot grill for about 1 minute until the dish begins to brown. Serve immediately, with warm granary bread and a side salad.

POTATO STICKS ★

This is a favourite way of mine of using up any leftover potato – they make crisp little goodies temptingly coated with caraway seeds. A delicious tea-time or supper-time snack which fills the kitchen with the lovely aromas of cheese and spice.

FOR 4

75 g (3 oz) cheese, finely grated	2 eggs, beaten
500 g (1 lb) potatoes, peeled, cooled and mashed	salt and pepper
	2 tablespoons caraway seeds

Add the grated cheese to the mashed potato and blend with all but a little of the beaten eggs. Season with salt and pepper and chill. Roll out on a lightly floured board to about 5 mm ($\frac{1}{4}$ inch) thick and cut into lengths 7 × 1 cm (3 × $\frac{1}{2}$ inch). Brush with the remaining egg and dust with caraway seeds. Bake in a preheated oven at 400°F/200°C/Gas 6 for 10 minutes, until brown and crisp.

NICE RICE SLICE ★

A couple of slices of this tasty loaf make an excellent snack meal – its base of rice is substantial and satisfying. It is also delicious cold, and can be successfully reheated.

FOR 4

4 eggs, separated	125 g (4 oz) Cheddar cheese, grated
600 ml (1 pint) milk	175 g (6 oz) rice, cooked
25 g (1 oz) margarine or butter, melted	salt and pepper

Beat the egg yolks and add to the milk, melted margarine or butter, and cheese. Mix into the rice and season with salt and pepper. Beat the whites until very stiff, fold into the mixture and bake in a 1 kg (2 lb) loaf tin in a preheated oven at 350°F/180°C/Gas 4 for 20–25 minutes. Cool for about 10 minutes before turning out.

MOP UP THE MUSHROOMS ★

So quick and simple to prepare, yet this snack is nutritious, delicious and satisfying. Served on toast, with some salads to go with it, it makes a marvellous light supper.

FOR 2

1 tablespoon grated onion
40 g (1½ oz) margarine or butter
125 g (4 oz) mushrooms, sliced
2 eggs, separated

50 g (2 oz) Cheddar cheese, grated
4 slices toast
salt and pepper

Cook the onion gently in the margarine or butter, and stir in the mushrooms. Cook for a minute or two, turning, until they begin to soften. Mix the egg yolks with the grated cheese and stir in the mushroom mixture. Beat the whites until very stiff and fold them in. Pile onto the toast and grill under a hot grill until puffed and golden.

MUSHROOM SCRAMBLE ★

A simple variation of scrambled eggs which is particularly popular with my tribe. I never overcook the eggs and try to keep them moist and creamy, slightly runny; the juices are delicious mopped up with fresh bread.

FOR 4

125 g (4 oz) button mushrooms, sliced
50 g (2 oz) margarine or butter
4 tablespoons milk

3 eggs, beaten
salt and pepper

Fry the sliced mushrooms in half of the butter or margarine. Melt the rest in a small saucepan and add the milk. Season the eggs with salt and pepper, and add them and the mushrooms to the milk. Stir until set. Put into a warm dish and serve with hot crusty bread.

POTATO PUFFS ★

In my experience potatoes are always popular with children, and with a little ingenuity you can make an immense variety of tasty goodies, all very economically – and as often as not using leftovers.

FOR 6

125 g (4 oz) Cheddar cheese, grated
450 ml (¾ pint) milk
750 g (1½ lb) potatoes, peeled, cooked
   and mashed
1 onion, finely chopped

salt and pepper
2 eggs, separated
1 egg, beaten
sesame seeds

Melt the cheese in the milk over a gentle heat and stir in the mashed potato and onion. Blend thoroughly and season to taste. Off the heat, stir in the egg yolks. Beat the whites very stiffly and fold into the mixture. Place in tablespoons on a well-greased baking tray and brush with beaten egg. Sprinkle with sesame seeds and bake in a preheated oven at 400°F/200°C/Gas 6 for 10–15 minutes.

COTTAGE OMELETTE ★

The device of blending cottage cheese to a purée is an excellent one, and makes a fabulous base for quiches as well as a super omelette filling. Mixed with spring onions, herbs and peas this is a popular, light meal with all the family – not least the cook!

FOR 4

250 g (8 oz) cottage cheese
1 small bunch spring onions, finely
   chopped
1 tablespoon mixed dried herbs
125 g (4 oz) peas, cooked

salt and pepper
6 eggs
4 tablespoons milk
vegetable oil for frying

Blend the cottage cheese to a smooth purée in the liquidizer. Mix in the spring onions, herbs and peas. Season to taste. Beat the eggs with the milk and season. Make the omelette in the usual way, using the cottage cheese and peas as the filling.

CHEESE FRITTERS

Treat-time. These melting morsels are wickedly delicious, rich and naughty, but none the less an essential part of childhood. (And pretty impossible for the grown-ups to resist, too.)

FOR 4

250 g (8 oz) **Gruyère cheese, cut into cubes**
vegetable oil for frying

FOR THE BATTER
125 g (4 oz) **plain flour**
a pinch of salt
3 tablespoons vegetable oil
150 ml ($\frac{1}{4}$ pint) warm water
1 egg white

To make the batter, sieve the flour with the salt and stir in the oil. Gradually add the water, stirring well until it is thick and creamy. Stand for 2 hours and then thin out with a little more water. Beat the egg white until very stiff and fold it into the batter just before you use it.

Dip the cheese cubes into the batter and deep-fry in very hot oil until the coating is puffed and golden all over, and the cheese is melting inside. Drain on kitchen paper and serve as soon as possible.

BEST MAC ★

Every cook has their favourite version of your actual macaroni cheese, and this is mine. It never fails and I have the satisfaction every time of seeing clean plates and happy faces!

FOR 4

250 g (8 oz) wholewheat macaroni or
  pasta shapes, cooked '*al dente*'
450 ml (¾ pint) béchamel (see page 14)
1 large onion, chopped
2 tablespoons dried herbs
50 g (2 oz) mushrooms, sliced

125 g (4 oz) peas, cooked and puréed
50 g (2 oz) cheese, grated
salt and pepper
25 g (1 oz) breadcrumbs
15 g (½ oz) Parmesan cheese, grated
15 g (½ oz) margarine or butter

Stir the cooked macaroni or pasta shapes into the béchamel, and then add the onion, herbs, vegetables and cheese. Season to taste with salt and pepper. Mix the breadcrumbs with the Parmesan and sprinkle over the top. Dot with margarine or butter and cook in a preheated oven at 350°F/180°C/Gas 4 for 12–15 minutes until bubbling and crisp on top.

POTATO DELIGHT ★

The idea for this dish came from the Auvergne where they make wonderful traditional cheese dishes with potatoes. The dry and crumbly Wensleydale that I use here begins to soak up the olive oil, and together they make a mouth-watering combination with tiny cubes of new potatoes.

FOR 4

500 g (1 lb) new potatoes, scrubbed
  and lightly steamed
4 tablespoons olive oil

75 g (3 oz) Wensleydale cheese, cubed
salt and pepper

Mix the potatoes with the olive oil and cheese and season with salt and pepper. Bake in an ovenproof dish in a preheated oven at 400°F/200°C/Gas 6 for about 15 minutes until sizzling. Delicious just with a green salad.

POTATO CHEESE PANCAKES ★

These are wonderful – a real treat, yet so cheap and easy to make. I find, though, that I never get to sit down and eat any – my role as cook is to fry them as fast as possible and dish them up at high speed! The kids behave like a nestful of gannets when these are around.

FOR 4

2 large potatoes, peeled and grated　　**2 eggs, beaten**
1 small onion, chopped　　**salt and pepper**
50 g (2 oz) Cheddar cheese, grated　　**vegetable oil for frying**

Rinse the grated potatoes and dry them thoroughly on a towel. Mix them with the onion, cheese and beaten eggs and season to taste. Heat the vegetable oil in a heavy pan and fry the mixture in large spoonfuls – about 10 cm (4 inches) in diameter – for 5 minutes on each side, so that the potatoes are cooked through and the pancakes golden brown.

PIP'S POTATOES ★

Wonderful evening food, and the potato comes into its own yet again. Its flavour comes through clearly, and the lightly cooked egg over the top makes this dish soft and delicious.

FOR 4

500 g (1 lb) new potatoes　　**salt and pepper**
2 medium onions, finely chopped　　**4 eggs**
75 g (3 oz) margarine or butter

Scrub the potatoes and slice them very finely. Mix with the onion, and cook gently in a heavy pan in all but 15 g ($\frac{1}{2}$ oz) of the butter or margarine, until soft. Season to taste and put into four individual heatproof dishes. Break an egg into each one and dot with the rest of the butter. Grill under a medium grill until the eggs are set. Serve immediately with crusty bread and a side salad.

IRISH EGGS

The veggie version of Scotch eggs – just as, if not more, delicious than their traditional sausagemeat coating. You could also use a good vegeburger mix instead of the fresh breadcrumbs just to vary this snack – which is delicious freshly cooked and served warm, and also excellent cold as picnic food.

FOR 4

1 tablespoon grated onion	1 egg, separated
1 teaspoon mixed dried herbs	salt and pepper
$\frac{1}{2}$ teaspoon dry mustard powder	4 hard-boiled eggs, shelled
75 g (3 oz) Cheshire or other dry cheese, grated	flour and dried breadcrumbs for coating
150 g (5 oz) fresh breadcrumbs	vegetable oil for frying

Mix the onion, herbs, mustard powder, cheese and fresh breadcrumbs with the egg yolk. Season to taste with salt and pepper. Pat out on to a lightly floured board and roll the eggs up in the mixture. Beat the egg white until very stiff, and roll the eggs in flour, egg white and breadcrumbs. Fry in very hot, deep oil until golden all over, about 8–10 minutes. Drain on kitchen paper.

YORKSHIRE DELIGHT

This is a version of that great family favourite, the Yorkshire pudding – but for vegetarians. The individual puddings are cooked so that they rise and hollow out in the middle, and they are then filled with a stuffing of your choice – creamed spinach is delicious, and so are any of the fillings in 'Croissant Stuffings and Toast Toppings'.

MAKES 15–18

125 g (4 oz) plain flour	300 ml ($\frac{1}{2}$ pint) milk
$\frac{1}{8}$ teaspoon salt	vegetable oil
1 egg	

Liquidize the flour, salt, egg and milk thoroughly together and leave to stand for an hour or two.

Pour a little vegetable oil into deep individual bun-tins and heat through in a preheated oven at 420°F/220°C/Gas 7 until it begins to smoke. Ladle 2 tablespoons of the mixture into each one and cook for 5–10 minutes, then turn the heat down to 375°F/190°C/Gas 5 for a further 15 minutes until cooked through.

Cool a little on a rack, then fill with your chosen filling.

CROISSANT STUFFINGS AND TOAST TOPPINGS *

Croissants are so delicious that it seems a shame only ever to have them for breakfast. Why not fill them with fillings that your children love, and serve them with salads, as a delightful and labour-saving supper? Likewise things on toast, or toasted sandwiches – for hurried lunches and late tea-times, and the days when you have had enough of sweating over the stove. Carefully thought out, these little meals can be perfectly nutritious, you don't have to rely on junk food, and they are amply satisfying – so use good wholemeal bread or granary and you are off to a flying start.

Purée of cottage cheese with grated Cheddar, chopped spring onions, and herbs
creamed mushrooms with grated Parmesan
purée of hot spinach with peas
leftover cauliflower cheese
Chinese stir-fry vegetables
peanut butter
creamed lettuce with watercress

apple slices fried in butter
tomatoes with chopped hard-boiled eggs and grated cheese
potted cheese
grated cheese mixed with butter and mustard, grilled
scrambled eggs with chopped spring onions

SMASHING SALAD SUGGESTIONS

Salads are a great area for improvisation, and very often the busy mother will throw all kinds of things into a salad depending on what is in the fridge at the time. So here are some simple outlines for salads to get that inspiration whirring. The individual touch, the proportion of ingredients used, is entirely up to you, according to the tastes of your family. And you can also use any dressing of choice – but see some of the ideas on pages 14–16.

BEAN SALADS *

Salads using cooked pulses are high in energy value, and provide substantial quantities of protein. They can be made to look as well as taste delicious, for beans and pulses cover a wide range of subtle colours, and mixed with things like sweetcorn and red peppers make salad dishes which are hard to resist.

1.
kidney beans, soaked and cooked (or canned)
aduki beans, soaked and cooked (or canned)
onion, very finely sliced
red cabbage, finely shredded
celery, finely sliced

2.
cannellini beans, soaked and cooked (or canned)
hard cheese such as Gruyère, cut into small cubes
iceberg lettuce, shredded
raw cauliflower florets, very finely sliced

3.
mung beans, soaked and cooked
small raw button mushrooms, quartered
French beans, steamed until tender and cut into 2.5 cm (1 inch) lengths
lettuce leaves

4.
butter beans, soaked and cooked (or canned)
sweetcorn, canned and drained
apple, cored and chopped small
celery, finely sliced

5.
aduki beans, soaked and cooked (or canned)
hard-boiled eggs, chopped
cucumber, peeled and cut into small dice
raw carrot, scrubbed and cut into julienne strips

PASTA SALADS ★

The majority of kids love pasta, and it is a good idea to introduce them to the idea of eating it in salads. The pasta soaks up the dressing of your choice (see pages 14–16) in a delicious way, and makes a versatile background for a wide variety of salad ingredients. Good, healthy food!

1.
pasta butterflies, cooked '*al dente*'
tiny raw cauliflower florets, very finely
   sliced
fresh mint leaves, chopped

2.
pasta twists, cooked '*al dente*'
cucumber, peeled, sliced and quartered
spring onions, chopped
smoked cheese, cut into cubes

3.
pasta bows, cooked '*al dente*'
cooked leeks, sliced and chopped
tomatoes, skinned and chopped

4.
pasta shells, cooked '*al dente*'
ripe avocado, cut into small dice
broccoli florets, steamed and cut small
banana, peeled, cut lengthwise and finely
   sliced

5.
penne, cooked '*al dente*'
peas, cooked '*al dente*'
cucumber, peeled and cut into cubes
watercress, chopped

RICE SALADS ★

Rice makes a nourishing and filling basis for salads, whether you use a tasty white rice like basmati, or the lovely nutty, crunchy brown rice. These all make lovely picnic salads, as well as being easily adaptable for salad dishes throughout the winter.

1.
rice, cooked until tender
canned sweetcorn, drained
tomatoes, skinned and chopped
spring onions, finely sliced

2.
brown rice, thoroughly cooked
runner beans, sliced very finely and cooked
cucumber, peeled and diced

3.
rice, cooked until nutty
celery, very thinly sliced
walnuts, chopped
watercress, chopped
white cabbage, grated

4.

rice, cooked until tender
baby carrots, scrubbed and finely sliced
raw mangetouts, shredded
almonds, skinned and chopped
oranges, peeled and chopped

5.

brown rice, cooked thoroughly
beansprouts
ripe avocado, peeled and diced
mixed nuts, chopped
lettuce, shredded

3.

raw button mushrooms, sliced
pasta shapes, cooked 'al dente'
spring onions, sliced
fresh herbs, finely chopped

4.

raw mushrooms, sliced
small French beans, cooked 'al dente'

5.

raw mushrooms, quartered
leeks, cooked and chopped
Gruyère cheese, cubed

MUSHROOM SALADS ★

Raw mushrooms are an excellent source of protein and are delicious in salads. These five combinations make highly popular salads with children.

1.

small button mushrooms, sliced
hard or smoked cheese, cut into small cubes
lettuce, shredded
hard-boiled egg, chopped
tomato, skinned and chopped

2.

small button mushrooms, quartered
ripe avocado, cut into small dice
lettuce heart leaves
fresh mint, chopped

FRUIT AND VEGETABLE SALADS ★

These should seduce the most unwilling of kids into eating healthy food; lovely combinations of sweet-tasting fresh fruit with crunchy vegetables will convert the most hardened of kids! The variations are of course infinite, but here are some ideas to start with!

1.

celery, sliced
potato, peeled, cooked and cubed
asparagus, cooked and cut into 2.5 cm
   (1 inch) lengths
tomato, skinned and chopped

2.

chicory leaves, cut into 2.5 cm (1 inch)
   lengths
walnuts, chopped
grapes, cut in half and seeded
apples, cored and chopped
oranges, peeled and cut up

3.

lettuce leaves
ripe avocado, sliced
plums, stoned and chopped
melon, balled or cubed
cottage cheese

4.

potatoes, peeled, cooked and diced
hard-boiled egg, chopped
apple, cored and chopped
raisins, stoned
fresh apricots, stoned and chopped

5.

carrots, grated
apple, cored and chopped
celery, finely chopped
peas, cooked 'al dente'
cucumber, peeled and diced
strawberries, hulled

6.

cabbage, finely shredded
cucumber, peeled and diced
dates, stoned and chopped

orange, peeled and chopped
spring onions, sliced
garlic croûtons (see page 16)

7.

cabbage, grated
pineapple, peeled and finely chopped
grapes, halved and seeded
chicory leaves, cut into 1 cm ($\frac{1}{2}$ inch) lengths
grated Parmesan

GREEN SALADS ★

Summery meals can be made fresh and inter-esting by the inclusion of a delicious green salad. There are so many variations of fresh lettuces and green vegetables to mix together during the summer months, and these salads go well with any of the main dishes in the previous chapters.

1.

cos, torn into short lengths
spring onions
mature Cheddar, grated
croûtons (see page 16)

2.

watercress, chopped
avocado, diced
beetroot, cooked and cut into julienne strips
celery, very finely sliced

3.

cabbage, very finely shredded
carrot, cut into julienne strips
fennel, cut into julienne strips
celery, grated

4.

lettuce leaves
celeriac, cut into julienne strips
hard-boiled egg, chopped
almonds, peeled, split and roasted

5.

chicory, cut into 5 mm ($\frac{1}{4}$ inch) rounds
cress
cucumber, peeled and diced
peas or petits pois, cooked until tender

6.

Chinese leaves, shredded
French beans, cooked and cut into 2.5 cm
    (1 inch) lengths
beansprouts
ripe avocado, diced

7.

cucumber, peeled and sliced into julienne
    strips
cabbage, grated
fennel, cut into julienne strips

8.

French beans, steamed and cut into 2.5 cm
    (1 inch) lengths
cheese, cubed
tomatoes, peeled and thinly sliced
lettuce heart leaves

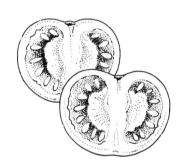

PERFECT
PICNICS

Children love picnics. The excitement of an unknown venue and expectations of exploring to find a sunlit place to sit and unpack the lunch basket are unique. So with all that anticipation, it is a treat to find something special inside it – tasty and colourful food that will make the day memorable

MUSHROOM AND EGG MAYONAISE ★

This combination of hard-boiled eggs and raw mushrooms with cubes of Wensleydale is particularly delicious if you dress it with the home-made mayonnaise on page 14. The flaked browned almonds, added at the last minutes, are a delicious finishing touch.

FOR 4

3 hard-boiled eggs, diced
175 g (6 oz) small button mushrooms, quartered
75 g (3 oz) Wensleydale cheese, diced

½ large iceberg lettuce, shredded
150 ml (¼ pint) sunflower oil mayonnaise (see page 14)
25 g (1 oz) flaked almonds, browned

Combine the eggs, mushrooms and cheese and toss with the lettuce. Dress with the mayonnaise, mixing thoroughly. Pack into a picnic box. Sprinkle the almonds over the top just before serving.

CHEESE LOAF

This is one of my most popular picnic recipes. You can make it plain if you like, or add chopped vegetables that your children are fond of – and it makes a lovely central point to a salady picnic.

FOR 6

250 g (8 oz) cottage cheese
75 g (3 oz) Cheddar cheese, finely
   grated
2 tablespoons mayonnaise (see
   page 14)
1 teaspoon moutarde de Meaux

1 tablespoon mixed dried herbs
2 tablespoons milk or single cream
15 g ($\frac{1}{2}$ oz) agar-agar, dissolved in 2
   tablespoons hot water
sliced cucumber, chopped stuffed
   olives etc (optional)

Liquidize the cottage cheese to a purée and mix in the grated cheese, mayonnaise, mustard and herbs. Thin out with the milk or cream and then fold in the dissolved agar-agar. Mix in the optional vegetables and leave to chill and set in a container. When ready to serve, run a knife around the sides to loosen the edges, and cut into slices in the container.

MUSHROOM SANDWICHES ★

When I first came across the idea for a mushroom sandwich I was, to say the least, sceptical. However, I tried them out and was immediately convinced. They make just about the best sandwich in the world – which is why I include them here.

Use fresh button mushrooms for the best results, slicing them thinly and sautéeing them lightly in a little oil so that they are cooked but still slightly crisp. Drain on kitchen paper and allow to cool. Then slice fresh granary bread, butter it, and sandwich with the sliced mushrooms. Press the bread slices well together and wrap in cling film until ready for use, keeping as cool as possible.

COLD OMELETTE CROUSTADES

Until I was given a cold omelette once on a picnic I did not believe that such a thing could be palatable – but made paper-thin, and rolled up, they are delicious. If the eggs are fresh and free-range, I find that there is no need to add fillings or to season them heavily – although of course you can easily do so to ring the changes.

FOR 4

6 eggs
5 tablespoons milk
salt and pepper
butter or margarine, softened

fillings of choice – herbs, creamed
**   mushrooms, spinach or sweetcorn**
**   (optional)**
1 long French loaf
cress, to garnish

Beat the eggs and pour in the milk, then continue beating for a few moments. Season to taste with salt and pepper and make four thin omelettes in the usual way, frying in some butter or margarine. Allow them to cool flat on a plate, and spread them with a filling if you choose to. Then roll them up quite tightly. Cut into diagonal slices.

Cut the loaf in half lengthwise down the middle and butter the cut edges. Cut it into four lengths. Place the omelette wheels on half of one 'sandwich' and cover with a sprinkling of cress. Cover with the top layer of bread and wrap in clingfilm until ready to use, keeping them as cool as possible.

FRIED EGG SANDWICHES

Another example of experience over expectation! It sounded too revolting, I thought, to slam a fried egg between wedges of bread and eat it stone-cold. But life is full of surprises, and when these are well-made they are delicious.

The secret is to fry the eggs very gently indeed, in oil, so that the yolk is not hard nor the white overcooked and crisp – so keep the heat down to moderate. Let the eggs cool on paper towels. Then slice fresh bread – wholemeal is particularly good – and butter the slices lightly. Sandwich with the cold eggs and wrap gently in clingfilm. These can be kept overnight in the fridge and are even better the following morning!

CAULIFLOWER TERRINE

A slice or two of this light, fresh terrine topped with sliced mushrooms makes an appetizing addition to a picnic lunch. It travels well so long as it is kept moderately cool, and I have found it to be popular with all age-groups of children.

FOR 4–5

1 medium cauliflower, cut into florets
2 small onions, chopped finely
herbs, garlic, etc (optional)
salt, pepper and nutmeg

125 g (4 oz) wholemeal breadcrumbs
4 eggs, beaten
50 g (2 oz) mushrooms, sliced

Steam the cauliflower until tender and reserve the water. Liquidize the florets with the onion, herbs and garlic (if used) and enough cooking liquid to bring it to a thin purée. Season to taste and stir in the breadcrumbs, again using the cooking water to thin out if necessary. Mix the beaten eggs, check the seasoning and pour into a well-greased loaf tin. Press the sliced mushrooms into the top and bake in a preheated oven at 400°F/200°C/Gas 6 for 35 minutes, then cool on a rack for 10–15 minutes. Turn out and wrap in clingfilm. Slice when ready to serve.

MOUSETRAP MOUSSE

A purée of cottage cheese with ripe avocado is the basis for this delicious mousse – and then little cubes of cucumber and smoked cheese are added with the other tasty morsels. It is the palest of greens, a delightful dish.

FOR 4–6

250 g (8 oz) cottage cheese
$\frac{1}{2}$ large, ripe avocado
6 spring onions, chopped
3 tablespoons parsley, chopped
salt and pepper
$\frac{1}{2}$ cucumber, peeled and diced

75 g (3 oz) smoked cheese, cubed (or
   half smoked cheese, half Cheddar)
3 tablespoons mayonnaise (see
   page 14)
15 g ($\frac{1}{2}$ oz) agar-agar, dissolved in
   2 tablespoons lemon juice

Purée the cottage cheese with the ripe avocado flesh in the blender until very smooth. Mix in the spring onions and parsley and season to taste with salt and pepper. Fold in the diced cucumber and cheese and stir in the mayonnaise. Finally mix in the agar-agar thoroughly, and pour into a well oiled ring-mould. Leave to chill and set for several hours or overnight.

GREEN PEA ROULADE

The sweetness of cooked lettuce with peas, puréed together and baked, makes a lovely roulade, inside which is a creamy, nutty filling. It looks sensational, yet it is easy to make if you follow the instructions carefully. I never believed that I'd ever be able to make a perfect roulade, but this one works a treat!

FOR 6–8

FOR THE ROULADE	FOR THE FILLING
1 medium lettuce, shredded	**5 tablespoons natural yogurt**
250 g (8 oz) peas, cooked	**175 g (6 oz) low-fat curd cheese**
1 tablespoon grated Parmesan cheese	**1 tablespoon dried mixed herbs**
salt, pepper and nutmeg	**75 g (3 oz) peanuts, coarsely ground**
3 eggs, beaten	

For the roulade, simmer the lettuce in a little water until soft, about 4–5 minutes. Drain thoroughly. Add to the peas, liquidize, then mix in the Parmesan. Season with salt, pepper and nutmeg. Mix into the beaten eggs and spread the mixture on to a 30 × 20 cm (12 × 8 inch) Swiss roll tin lined with a sheet of greaseproof paper. Bake in a preheated oven at 400°F/200°C/Gas 6 for 25 minutes until risen and set. Cool a little for 5–10 minutes.

For the filling, mix the yogurt with the curd cheese, herbs and ground peanuts. Turn out the roulade base on to another sheet of greaseproof paper and gently peel off the back lining paper. Spread the filling over the top and roll up. Chill, and wrap in clingfilm. Serve sliced.

STUFFED TOMATOES ★

There are many variations on the theme, of course, but this creamy, nutty and herby mixture is one of the simplest to prepare. Lovely in high summer when tomatoes are plentiful and herbs at their best.

FOR 4

4 medium tomatoes
250 g (8 oz) low-fat cream cheese
2 tablespoons milk
50 g (2 oz) walnuts, chopped

1 tablespoon chives, finely chopped
1 tablespoon parsley, finely chopped
salt and pepper

Cut the tomatoes in half around the middle and scoop out the flesh. Mash the cream cheese with the milk and mix in the chopped walnuts and herbs. Season to taste with salt and pepper and stuff the mixture into the hollowed-out tomatoes. Pack into a picnic box, cover with foil, and chill.

CHEESE SALAD SPECIAL ★

This is one of the best of picnic salads – a mixture of vegetables with the mouth-watering addition of croûtons and three different kinds of cheese. It makes quite a substantial dish so it saves you making a multitude of other salads!

FOR 4

croûtons (see page 16), omitting the
    garlic
1 large cos lettuce
125 g (4 oz) radishes, sliced
1 box cress
8 spring onions, sliced

75 g (3 oz) hard cheese, diced
75 g (3 oz) smoked cheese, diced
15 g ($\frac{1}{2}$ oz) Parmesan cheese, grated
5 tablespoons vinaigrette (see
    page 14), stored in an airtight jar

Make the croûtons, drain and cool them, then store in an airtight jar.

Tear the lettuce leaves into about 7.5 cm (3 inch) lengths and mix in all the rest of the salad ingredients. Toss in the diced cheeses and the Parmesan. Pack into a picnic box to keep cool and crisp. Just before serving add the croûtons and toss in the vinaigrette.

CHARLIE BROWN'S FLAN

Peanuts are the point of this flan, hence its title – and it deserves to be as famous as its namesake. It is a delectable mixture of layers – onion, mushrooms and cheese, with a thick layer of chopped peanuts over the top.

FOR 4

2 medium onions, sliced
4 tablespoons vegetable oil
1 × 20 cm (8 inch) pastry pie shell,
    baked blind
125 g (4 oz) mushrooms, sliced
1 small bunch parsley, finely chopped
125 g (4 oz) cheese, grated
125 g (4 oz) peanuts, chopped

Soften the onion in half the oil over a gentle heat, covered, stirring occasionally, for 8–10 minutes. Make a layer of onion in the base of the flan case. Sauté the mushrooms in the remaining oil so that they are half-cooked and still crisp. Mix with the parsley and place on top of the onion. Top this with the grated cheese and finally cover with the chopped peanuts. Bake at 325°F/160°C/Gas 3 for 30 minutes. Allow to cool on a rack.

SUMMERY TOMATO FLAN ★

For all its simplicity this is one of the best of picnic flans. The purée base of cottage cheese makes it a little different from the normal quiche and it is light and tasty, delicious with fresh bread and salads.

FOR 4–6

250 g (8 oz) cottage cheese
3 eggs, beaten
2 tablespoons mixed dried herbs
1 small bunch spring onions, chopped

salt and pepper
1 × 25 cm (10 inch) crispy pastry case (see page 13), baked blind
4 medium tomatoes, sliced

Purée the cottage cheese in the blender and then pour in the beaten eggs and liquidize again. Stir in the herbs and spring onions and season to taste with salt and pepper. Pour into the prepared pastry shell and cover with the slices of tomato. Bake in a preheated oven at 375°F/190°C/Gas 5 for 30–35 minutes until set. Cool on a rack.

PANCAKE PIZZA

These pizzas make marvellous picnic fare. Tasty, aromatic and colourful, they are always popular with children. The pancake base is a little different from the normal pizza, and makes a thick, light background to a mouth-watering filling.

MAKES 3 PIZZAS

FOR THE PANCAKES

150 g (5 oz) wholewheat flour
2 large eggs, separated
150 ml ($\frac{1}{4}$ pint) milk and water mixed
1 tablespoon oil

FOR THE FILLING

1 × 200 g (7 oz) can tomatoes, drained and sliced

2 large onions, sliced
3 tablespoons oil
50 g (2 oz) Mozzarella cheese, sliced thinly
125 g (4 oz) mushrooms, thinly sliced and sautéed in a little oil
1 tablespoon dried thyme
salt and pepper
25 g (1 oz) Parmesan cheese, grated

For the pancakes, liquidize the flour with the egg yolks, milk, water and oil. Allow it to rest for 2 hours. Then beat the egg whites stiffly and fold into the batter. Cook one-third of the mixture in a large, heavy frying pan, making one at a time, for 2–3 minutes on each side so that they are cooked through and golden. Cool on kitchen paper.

For the filling, lay the tomatoes on to the prepared bases. Sauté the onions gently in the oil until soft, about 10 minutes, and place over the top. Cover with the Mozzarella slices and the mushrooms, sprinkle with thyme and season with salt and pepper. Sprinkle with the grated Parmesan and bake in a preheated oven at 350°F/180°C/Gas 4 for 20 minutes. Allow to cool, and store stacked between layers of foil in a plastic box.

COLOURFUL PIE

There is something delightfully old-fashioned about this pie: it has a pronouncedly home-baked look about it, and when you slice through the pastry you see a lovely combination of colours – yellow, red and green – which is immediately appetizing.

FOR 4–6

250 g (8 oz) blender pastry (see page 13)
1 medium onion, sliced
2 tablespoons vegetable oil
1 × 400 g (14 oz) can sweetcorn, drained
4 tomatoes, skinned and chopped
2 leeks, cooked and sliced

50 g (2 oz) peas, cooked
50 g (2 oz) cheese, grated
salt and pepper
beaten egg

Roll out two-thirds of the pastry and line a well oiled 20 cm (8 inch) pie dish. Soften the onion in the oil and mix into the sweetcorn. Add the tomatoes, leeks, peas and cheese and season to taste with salt and pepper. Fill the pie shell and cover with the rest of the pastry, sealing the edges together with water and pressing down with a fork. Brush with beaten egg and bake in a preheated oven at 375°F/190°C/Gas 5 for 15–20 minutes until the pastry is set and golden. Cool and chill.

COTTAGE CHEESE MOUSSES ★

Light little mouthfuls for a summery day, these mousses travel well (so long as they are kept cool), and they make a lovely centrepiece to a salady picnic.

FOR 4

250 g (8 oz) cottage cheese
4 tablespoons natural yogurt
1 tablespoon chopped fresh mint
125 g (4 oz) French beans, cut into
   5 mm ($\frac{1}{4}$ inch) lengths

50 g (2 oz) peanuts, chopped
salt and pepper
15 g ($\frac{1}{2}$ oz) agar-agar dissolved in 3
   tablespoons lemon juice

Purée the cottage cheese thoroughly with the yogurt. Stir in the mint, French beans and nuts, and season to taste with salt and pepper. Mix in the dissolved agar-agar. Put into four individual ramekin dishes and chill until set.

WATERCRESS ROLL ★

The freshness of watercress makes a wonderful basis for this loaf, and a few walnuts mixed in gives it a crunch and contrast both of texture and of taste. Lovely picnic food.

FOR 4

250 g (8 oz) low-fat cream cheese
50 g (2 oz) Cheddar cheese, grated
2 tablespoons milk
2 bunches watercress, washed and
   finely chopped

125 g (4 oz) walnuts, chopped
1 onion, finely chopped
salt and pepper

Mash the cheeses with the milk until smooth – or blend in the food processor. Mix in the watercress, walnuts and onion, and season to taste. Shape into a roll and place on greaseproof paper. Wrap it up securely and pat smooth. Chill, and serve sliced.

PARTY
TIME

When it comes to party time it is hard to stick to your principles about healthy eating! The traditional kids' party consists of a table groaning with foods which are more likely to poison the children than to give them the vitality they need to cope with all the excitement. There is a school of thought that many of the additives in 'instant' foods and others provoke or promote hyperactivity in children. So if the kids behave badly it may not be altogether their fault! By trying some of these ideas you will be cutting down on the additive element in party foods, and also giving pleasure to the kids whose sensibilities are outraged by what goes into that sausage on a stick . . .

SPECIAL SANDWICHES

Sandwiches play an obvious and ubiquitous part on the tea-time table, but there are many variations on the ordinary theme: toasted sandwiches, made in a sandwich-maker, are delicious and easy to make, and you can fill them with all sorts of tempting (and healthy!) fillings. You can also bake sandwiches, or dip them in beaten egg or milk and lightly fry them in vegetable oil to make a more substantial dish of them. You can actually be creative with sandwiches! Cut them into attractive shapes, or use brown and white bread in one sandwich, or nut spreads instead of butter.... You and your kids will soon discover that a sandwich need not be a predictable or boring part of a festive table.

Toasted sandwiches

Butter the outsides only of the sandwiches, fill with your chosen filling and pop into the sandwich-maker for 3–4 minutes until golden and crisp. You can also toast them under a grill, but this is not such a tidy operation as using a special toaster which seals the edges together (and the filling in). When you turn a sandwich under the grill it tends to collapse on you – so baking it is a better bet if you do not possess a sandwich-maker.

HOT BAKED SANDWICHES

To bake sandwiches, make them in the usual way with the filling of your choice, and then lightly butter the outsides. Bake in a preheated oven at 350°F/180°C/Gas 4 for 6–8 minutes just so that the sandwiches begin to crisp up, then serve immediately.

POOR KNIGHTS

This is the traditional name for a humble dish which is nonetheless warming, nutritious and delicious. Make your sandwiches as normal, then dip them in beaten egg and milk and quickly fry them in hot, light vegetable oil until they are crisp and golden on both sides. Drain on kitchen paper and serve as soon as possible.

PARTY LOAF

Cut the crusts off a large sandwich loaf and slice it lengthwise into 5 mm (¼ inch) slices. Spread these slices with nut butter and fill with a salad filling dressed with mayonnaise. Reconstitute the loaf, wrap it in cling-film and refrigerate under a plate to weight it down and compress it. When chilled and slightly flattened, cut downwards in slices.

PINWHEELS ★

Cut the crusts off large slices of bread, spread them with your chosen filling and roll them up. Chill, then cut crosswise into wheels.

Zebras ★

Use white and wholemeal bread together in one sandwich, so that one side is white and the other is brown.

Hot Buttered Fingers

For kids with very simple tastes, this is a delicious alternative to hot buttered toast. Simply slice the bread that you like to use into normal slices, and butter them. Cook at 300°F/150°C/Gas 2 for 20–25 minutes until golden and crisp. Cool a little before serving.

Savoury Sandwich Fillings

Sliced cheese and tomato
cream cheese and chutney
thin slivers of apple with cheese
raw tomatoes and soft cheese
scrambled eggs flavoured with
  Marmite
mushrooms with sunflower spread

purée of hard-boiled egg, watercress
  and mayonnaise
purée of butter beans and skinned
  tomatoes
Marmite and chopped dry-roasted
  peanuts

Felafels ★

MAKES ABOUT 12

500 g (1 lb) canned chick peas, drained
1 onion, peeled and grated
salt and pepper

1 egg yolk
wholemeal flour
vegetable oil, for frying

Purée the chickpeas. Stir in the grated onion and season to taste, then mix in the beaten egg yolk thoroughly. Chill. Fry tablespoons of the mixture, rolled in wholemeal flour, in oil until golden on both sides, about 8–10 minutes in all.

Nut Spread Sandwich Fillings

A liberal spreading of these makes a simple but simply delicious hot sandwich. You can also make delicious spreads for covering breads, savoury biscuits or filling sandwiches, using hazelnuts, walnuts, Brazil nuts, pine nuts or almonds – all lightly grilled until they turn brown as for the sunflower spread below. Liquidize with melted butter using the same quantities of each, and season as you wish with garlic, herbs and spices, according to your family's taste.

HOME-MADE CRUNCHY PEANUT BUTTER 1

175 g (6 oz) dry roasted peanuts, coarsely ground

175 g (6 oz) margarine or butter, melted

Add the ground peanuts to the melted fat and mix well. Pack down into a container and chill.

HOME-MADE CRUNCHY PEANUT BUTTER 2

250 g (8 oz) raw peanuts

125 g (4 oz) margarine or butter, melted

In a coffee grinder, liquidize half the peanuts with their skins on, to a fine powder. Stir into the melted fat and then add the remaining nuts, coarsely ground. Mix well and pack down into a container.

SUNFLOWER SPREAD

125 g (4 oz) sunflower seeds

125 g (4 oz) margarine or butter

Grill the sunflower seeds under a moderate grill, shaking from time to time, until they turn brown all over. Melt the fat and liquidize with the toasted seeds. Put into a container and chill.

Sweet Sandwich Fillings

Lemon curd	strawberry jam with toasted almonds
sliced kiwi fruit	sliced banana with marmalade
mashed banana	honey with chopped walnuts.

APRICOT DELIGHT

125 g (4 oz) dried apricots, soaked	60 ml (2 fl oz) fresh orange juice

Liquidize the soaked, drained apricots with the juice to a thick purée. Store in the refrigerator for up to 3 days.

PARTY SNACKS

Home-made Crisps and Crisplets

You can make your own version of the ever-popular potato crisp at far less cost than the shop-shelf variety – and it is also far more delicious. These home-made goodies seem to have some resemblance to the potato from which they are claimed to originate, and at least you have the certain knowledge of what has or has not gone into them! For the deep-frying use a light vegetable oil such as sunflower or groundnut, and drain the crisps immediately on kitchen paper so that they are dry and crunchy, not oily and soggy.

Peel medium potatoes and slice them into very thin slivers – using the slicer on the side of the cheese grater is the best way I have found of doing this. Pat the slices dry with a clean cloth and deep-fry in very hot oil until they are golden and crisp. Drain and dry on kitchen paper and keep warm.

You can also make CRISPLETS. These are made in the same way as the crisps but using coarsely grated potato instead of slices. Stir them while frying so that they separate from each other. The crisplets make wonderful golden nibbles, and store well in airtight jars if you are fortunate enough to have any left over!

Little Jackets

Deep-fried skins of jacket potatoes are simply delicious: just bake your potatoes in the normal way ($1\frac{1}{4}$ hours in a preheated oven at 400°F/200°C/Gas 6), cut them in half and scoop the potato flesh out. (You can use this for the Potato Pastry on page 13.) Chop the skins into little squares and deep-fry them in very hot oil until crisp. Drain and dry on kitchen paper and keep warm until ready to serve. They are also delicious as a cold snack, and can be used to dip into dips.

Deep-Fried Rice

This is another recipe which, like the little jackets, is fantastically mouth-watering for something so simple and so cheap. Using cold, leftover cooked rice, separate the grains a little so that they are not in big clusters, and deep-fry in very hot oil until golden all over. Drain and dry on kitchen paper. Sprinkle with a little sea salt and allow to cool. They are crunchy and extremely more-ish – and if you do have any leftovers they store well in an airtight jar.

Toasted Sunflower Seed Medley

For all its simplicity this is an outstanding snack – really delicious, and of course highly nutritious. Just grill sunflower seeds, pumpkin seeds, and sesame seeds under a moderate grill, shaking from time to time so that they brown evenly. Cool and store in airtight jars.

You can use the same method for peeled almonds, hazelnuts, pine nuts or Brazils – they are all transformed in taste by the light grilling, and make delicious morsels which are far better for your children's health than processed snacks full of colourings and preservatives. Mix them together with some raisins and dried bananas and it makes an excellent snack.

POPCORN SPECIAL ★

Instead of coating home-popped popcorn with something sweet, try tossing it in a mixture of malt extract and Marmite – 1 tablespoon malt extract and 2 tablespoons Marmite to every 25 g (1 oz) uncooked popcorn. Or you can sprinkle the popcorn with celery salt or garlic salt for a simpler snack.

CHEESE SURPRISES

Wrap little cubes of Cheddar in rice paper and seal them by pressing down the moistened edges. Deep-fry in very hot oil until the rice paper is crisp and the cheese inside melted – about 1 minute. Drain and cool a little before serving.

PEANUT SQUARES ★

These light little biscuits melt in the mouth, and a plateful invariably vanishes at party-time!

MAKES 16

125 g (4 oz) plain flour
125 g (4 oz) margarine

125 g (4 oz) Cheddar cheese, finely grated
50 g (2 oz) peanuts, coarsely ground

Blend the flour, margarine and cheese to a thick paste. Roll out on a floured board to about 5 mm ($\frac{1}{4}$ inch) thick. Sprinkle the ground peanuts over the top and press them into the dough, then cut into 5 cm (2 inch) squares. Bake on a well-greased baking tray in a preheated oven at 375°F/190°C/Gas 5 for 15 minutes. Cool on a rack.

PARTY CENTREPIECES

PARTY DIP ★

1 large carton natural yogurt   1 packet dried onion soup

Mix the two together and put into a pretty bowl. Surround with raw vegetables cut into thin strips to dip – carrots, celery, cucumber and cauliflower – and also little fingers of dry toast, and Little Jackets (see page 87).

NUTTY DIP ★

1 × 250 g (8 oz) can cannellini beans,   4–6 tablespoons olive oil
   drained   sea salt and pepper
250 g (8 oz) crunchy peanut butter (see
   page 85)

Liquidize the beans, peanut butter and oil together, and season to taste with sea salt and pepper. Thin out if necessary with more oil. Serve with sliced raw mushrooms, and other vegetables arranged attractively around the bowl.

VOL-AU-VENTS GALORE ★

Cook puff pastry vol-au-vents from frozen as instructed on the packet. Cool them on a rack, and fill with any of the fillings below, or with one of the following:
1. Browned flaked almonds, raw courgettes cubed small, mixed into mayonnaise (see page 14).
2. Finely chopped celery and sunflower seeds mixed into blue-cheese mayonnaise (see page 15).

LITTLE BOXES

Cut the crusts off a large sandwich loaf, then cut the bread into 7 cm (3 inch) cubes. Very carefully hollow out each cube with a sharp knife, taking care not to break the sides of the box. Deep-fry in very hot oil until golden, then drain and dry on kitchen paper. Leave to cool. Fill with puréed creamed mushrooms (see page 50), or creamy scrambled eggs either hot or cold. The variations are endless – and you can also fill the boxes with any of the fillings on page 84.

LIGHT PUFF-PASTRY ROLLS

Roll puff pastry out thinly. Cut into little rectangles about 5 × 10 cm (2 × 4 inches). Place a filling of choice on the surface and roll up, sealing the bottom edge with water and pressing it down with a fork. Brush with beaten egg and scatter with either sesame or poppy seeds. Bake in a pre-heated oven at 400°F/200°C/Gas 6 for 8–10 minutes until puffed and golden.

Or you can make very small Cheese Triangles (see page 36).

FILLINGS

Sliced mushrooms, mixed with a little curd cheese and bound with egg yolk

grated cheese, mixed and bound similarly

chopped spring onions in cream cheese, bound with beaten egg

drained canned sweetcorn, bound with curd cheese and egg yolk

packet vegeburger mix or sos-mix, made up as instructed

CANAPÉS

Make up a platter of different canapés all based on squares of fried bread. Try making the rolled omelettes on page 73 and cutting them into wheels, and putting each one on a square of the fried bread. You can also spear cubes of apple and cheese on to them, or little squares of Brie with pineapple, or a mixture of herbed cream cheese with grapes. Lightly steamed button mushrooms, cooled, make a simple but delicious canapé, too.

SUNBURGERS ★

MAKES 8

1 medium onion, finely chopped
vegetable oil
250 g (8 oz) sunflower seeds, blended
   to a powder in the coffee grinder
175 g (6 oz) carrots, finely grated

1 egg
salt, pepper and dried herbs
oatmeal

Fry the onion in a little oil for a few minutes until softened. Mix with the seed powder, carrots and egg, season to taste, and shape into eight mini-burgers. Roll in oatmeal and fry in more oil for about 8 minutes on each side, until brown and crisp all over.

DAVY CROCKETS

MAKES 8

1 large onion, peeled and chopped
vegetable oil
175 g (6 oz) lentils or aduki beans,
   soaked and cooked (see page 12)
125 g (4 oz) mushrooms, sliced and
   chopped

herbs, salt and pepper, to taste
1 beaten egg, to bind
oatmeal

Sauté the onion in a little oil until soft and mix into the cooked pulses. Purée in the liquidizer and mix in the mushrooms. Season to taste and chill. Shape into eight croquettes and coat in beaten egg and oatmeal. Fry in vegetable oil until golden all over, about 10 minutes in all.

BABY PIZZA SQUARES ★

Make the scone pizza on page 31, using a square tin to bake it in. Cool, then cut into little squares – they disappear like hot cakes!

Menu Planner

Here are some ideas for entire meals which include recipes from throughout the book, and which aim to provide well-balanced meals. The puddings are simple ones, for which many cooks have their favourite recipes, and most of which in any case can be found in basic cookery books. Other meals are rounded off with yogurt or fresh fruit, giving the cook a welcome break!

LUNCHES

Bubbling Casserole
Tempting Cabbage   Green Salad
Bread and Butter Pudding

Merry Mushroom Loaf
Cunning Carrots   Crunchy Potatoes
Fruit Salad

Topping Tomato Layers
Lentil Stirabout   Mushroom Salad
Apricot and Prune Compôte

Leek Pasties with Mushroom Sauce
Oatmeal Tomatoes   Fruit and Vegetable
   Salad
Baked Bananas

Crunchy Croustades
Nutty Cabbage   Rice Salad
Rhubarb Fool

Savoury Spring Rolls
Mushroom Munch   Bean Salad
Gooseberry Crumble

Noodle Doodle
Corn Fritters   Mixed Green Salad
Cheesecake with Prunes

Tomato Charlotte
Sesame Potato Cakes   Bean Salad
Chocolate Mousse

Gâteau di Patate
Crusty Broccoli and Mushroom Bake
Fruit and Vegetable Salad
Blackcurrant Meringue

Best Cheese Pie
Grated Potato Hash   Green Salad
Lemon Sponge Pudding

Mushroom Cobbler
Grated Potato Pancakes   Rice Salad
Treacle Tart

Elegant Egg Flan
Cheesy Roast Potatoes   Mixed Salad
Bread and Butter Pudding

SUPPERS

Cheese Soup with granary bread
Pasta Salad   Mushroom Salad
Fresh Fruit and Yogurt

Best Mac
Oatmeal Tomatoes
Fruit and Vegetable Salad
Baked Bananas

Pip's Potatoes
Fruit and Vegetable Salads
Cheeseboard

Vegemites' Spaghetti
Green Salad
Bananas in Yogurt

Super Supper Slice
Mushroom Salads
Fresh Fruit

Swiss Bliss
Sesame Potato Cakes
Mushroom Salad
Fresh Fruit

Secret Soup with granary rolls
Cottage Omelette   Green Salad
Oranges in Yogurt

Puffy Soufflé
Potato Delight
Bean Salad
Baked Apples

Scone Pizza
Bean Salads
Fresh Fruit

Rosemary's Risotto
Green Salad
Yogurt

Golden Sweetcorn Soup with fresh
    wholemeal bread
Mushroom Scramble
Rice Salad
Yogurt

Crispy Plate Pancakes
Lentil Stirabout
Fruit and Vegetable Salad
Grated Apple in Yogurt

INDEX

INDEX